CHATHAM HOUSE PAPERS · 42

BRITISH SPACE POLICY AND INTERNATIONAL COLLABORATION

James Eberle and Helen Wallace

The Royal Institute of International Affairs

Routledge & Kegan Paul
London, New York and Andover

First published 1987
by Routledge & Kegan Paul Ltd
11 New Fetter Lane, London EC4P 4EE
29 West 35th Street, New York, NY 10001, USA, and
North Way, Andover, Hants SP10 5BE

Set, printed and bound by
Stephen Austin and Sons Ltd, Hertford

ISBN 0-7102-1365-4

CONTENTS

ABBREVIATIONS

BAe	British Aerospace
BNSC	British National Space Centre
Brite	Basic Research in Industrial Technologies for Europe
BTI	British Telecom International
CERN	European Centre for Nuclear Research
Copuos	Committee on the Peaceful Uses of Outer Space (UN)
DBS	Direct broadcasting (by) satellite
DoD	US Department of Defense
DTI	Department of Trade and Industry
EC	European Community
ELDO	European Launcher Development Organization
ESA	European Space Agency
Esprit	European Strategic Programme for Research and Development in Information Technology
ESRO	European Space Research Organization
ITU	International Telecommunications Union
MOD	Ministry of Defence
MSS	Marconi Space Systems
Nasa	National Aeronautics and Space Administration
Nato	North Atlantic Treaty Organization
NERC	Natural Environment Research Council
PTT	Postes Télégraphes Téléphones
SERC	Science and Engineering Research Council
Star	Special Telecommunications Action for Regional Development

PREFACE

Over the past two years space policy has been the subject of review in Britain. In parallel the European Space Agency has been clarifying its long-term proposals, negotiations have been under way with the United States over the international space station and a debate has started on how far Europeans should collaborate in space to enhance their security. The issues raised for Western Europe as a whole are covered in *Europe's Future in Space: A Joint Policy Report* (Chatham House Special Paper), in which this institute joined four sister European institutes to produce a common appraisal.

This paper focuses on the British dimension and the specific British interests which are relevant to decisions about future space policy. As we went to press British policy hung on the final round of decision-making in Cabinet, assisted by the new Advisory Council on Science and Technology. Whatever the outcome we hope that this paper serves both to document the debate and to spell out the implications of the different options under discussion.

Throughout the preparation of this paper we have been helped by the constant support, willing tutoring and critical commentary of many British space experts. Friends from the British National Space Centre and other parts of government, from across the industry including producers of space systems and subsystems (British Aerospace, Marconi Space Systems, Logica, Thorn-EMI and others) and the operators of services, especially British Telecom International, and independent experts, including Keith Hayward, Mahindra Naraine, and Geoffrey Pardoe all have contributed to this paper in

Preface

different ways. But we, as authors, of course bear the responsibility for the text itself and the opinions which it expresses.

This paper was written for the West European Programme of the institute, which has core funding from the Gatsby Charitable Trust. Its production owes much to the staff of the institute, in particular Margaret Beringer, Marie Lathia, Nigel Pearce and Pauline Wickham and ever-assiduous colleagues in the Library and Press Library.

October 1987   J.E.
                                                                                          H.W.

SUMMARY

Space activities have too long been looked upon as just another area of esoteric research and development, the practical applications of which could be left to the superpowers. In neither the civilian nor the military field has British policy traditionally taken into account the wide-ranging relevance of space technology for the economy, society, foreign policy or security. Instead policy-makers have looked narrowly at those individual space programmes which might be useful for rather specific scientific, industrial or military purposes. In short there have been decisions but no policy.

This narrow approach contrasts sharply with the policies of most of the other technologically advanced nations which have chosen to invest seriously in space. For them space policy has been defined as a necessary domain in which they could not afford not to invest. American and Soviet efforts are well known. Rather more relevant is the fact that Japan and India as well as China have dynamic space programmes, while within Europe not only France, the European pioneer, but Germany and Italy have overtaken British levels of involvement in space.

So far Britain has been relatively lucky. An inherited ability in science and engineering and the determination of a few companies have enabled Britain to develop strengths in some space activities, notably in telecommunications and scientific research. The European Space Agency has proved a rewarding framework for collaboration, from which Britain has derived real dividends. On the military side Britain has been able to make some use of space technology directly through the Skynet programme and Nato satellites and indirectly through privileged access to US sources of satellite data.

But this mix of capabilities is not sufficient to sustain Britain as a serious actor in space. Technologies change fast and industrial competitiveness depends on the ability to keep up with the pace of innovation. Markets are immature, except in the established sector of telecommunications, and most are either protected by public procurement practices or subject to other political pressures. It is not possible to contribute effectively to the space business at either government or company level except by international collaboration. And collaboration is a two-way street which requires sustained commitments from all of the partners. Furthermore the scale and character of investment needed means there is some degree of risk involved, risk which it makes sense to share with partners from other countries.

Meanwhile developments in the military field are making space technologies increasingly relevant to security policy. As long as Britain retains its nuclear capability it has particular need of data from satellites to assist deployment and targeting as well as to assess capabilities. If arms control and a measure of disarmament are to be achieved, it is vital to be able to monitor and verify, for which satellites are an invaluable source of information. British policy-makers have to think carefully about how far existing capabilities will serve these two needs. They must consider what balance of European, American and national resources makes most sense.

For all of these reasons Britain needs a space policy. To this end the British National Space Centre (BNSC) was created in 1985. Its strategic plan advocated a major expansion of investment and activities in the civilian field. This was aimed at improving national capabilities, but in the knowledge that the European Space Agency (ESA) was about to reach a collective decision on Europe's long-term programmes. Britain's place within that programme would have to be established. Once the ESA decisions were reached there would be little opportunity for second and third thoughts.

BNSC's contribution to the policy debate has been a welcome improvement on the fragmented approach which had preceded. But it has only succeeded in going part of the way towards a strategy. The defence and civilian dimensions are still not integrated, a major weakness in a sector where the same technologies and often the same missions and satellites serve both civilian and military purposes. Nor is BNSC strong enough as an agency to achieve the targeted assessment of objectives, funding and programmes which has been possible in those countries where a strategic approach is more deeply rooted.

Four scenarios can be envisaged for the future. A *significant expansion*, broadly as advocated by BNSC, would produce a larger national capability, the opportunity for an effective role in Europe and the option of an increased military effort. Britain could at a lower level of increase have a *serious but selective* involvement in space, building up further strengths in those priority areas deemed most useful for economic and security needs. To hold to the *status quo* in terms of the level and character of activities would almost certainly mean to drop back, given the pace of movement in the space sector and likely international developments. As an alternative to all of these, Britain could reconcile itself to being a *user but not a major producer* of space technology, dependent on suppliers and innovators abroad.

Whichever outcome emerges from the current review will have major and long-term implications. These go well beyond issues of research and development or the concerns of a specialist scientific community and a few companies. Space policy touches directly on British interests across the range of economic competitiveness, technological innovation, international influence and relationships with both American and European partners.

1
INTRODUCTION

Space science and technology have over the last three decades opened up remarkable new opportunities for understanding our universe and for serving very practical human needs. The further potential is enormous, but to harness it requires both sustained investment and coherent international collaboration. The United States and the Soviet Union have long dominated the search to exploit space technologies, their interest fuelled by their global military requirements as well as their civilian needs.

The West Europeans, after a shaky start, have developed an impressive capability in space, articulated so far largely through the European Space Agency (ESA). That Western Europe and ESA have achieved so much is largely due to the pioneering efforts of France, where there has been a consistent determination to promote space programmes. This determination is now increasingly shared by policy-makers elsewhere in the world. Japan is on course to establish itself as the world's no.3 in space. China and India have ambitious programmes. Other countries such as Brazil are in the process of developing space capabilities. The belief which fuels this burst of activities is that technological prowess, economic advancement, political standing and security will in the 21st century require an active presence in space.

But few countries can aspire to this on their own. The USA and the USSR may have achieved much from their own huge resources, though both have also been significantly engaged in international space cooperation. The Chinese, more modestly, have a largely

1

independent programme. For all other countries some form of international collaboration has been and remains an absolute prerequisite. ESA has established a wide-ranging programme only by virtue of its success in welding together a collective European approach for the civilian use of space. Nor can any country, even a superpower, operate in space without mechanisms to impose a degree of international regulation and management. For some years efforts have been under way through the United Nations to develop a global space regime. Many functional areas of space technology are now regulated to greater or lesser effect by specialized international agencies or consortia. There are no real choices about whether to collaborate. The crucial policy questions are about how to collaborate and with whom.

Why space technology matters
It must be made clear at the outset that space technology is not just another area of technology which deserves public or private investment. It occupies an unusual position at the frontiers of science and technology as a driver for many other areas of potential advancement, both technological and economic. Two analogies serve to reinforce this point. First, in the 1920s the development of the aeroplane was the subject of interesting but detached speculation. The British Navy saw 'no use for planes' and there were no markets to lead the suppliers to produce. Yet hindsight reveals just how important aviation was to prove for both military and civilian purposes. And the ability to travel long distances quickly by air brought in its train unimagined political, economic, social and military changes. Second, the automobile industry is acknowledged to have played the role of multiplier in the 1950s and 1960s, drawing in its wake advances in steel, glass, rubber, machine tools, and opening up investment and employment across the transport sector. Over the next decade and beyond space technology and the state of its art offer a promising combination of innovation and spin offs. Its character as a leading edge technology makes it possible to expect benefits to follow, though impossible to predict their extent or value.

In the companion European volume to this paper the arguments for the relevance of space technology to international and domestic policy are set out at length and in considerable detail. Readers interested in following through the many applications of space technology, both current and potential, will find much valuable material to quarry. The companion volume also describes and assesses the capabilities of the major and burgeoning space powers in the international arena. A thorough account is provided there of the European record, along with a critical appraisal of its strengths and weaknesses. The key points covered in that volume are summarized here in the context of their specific relevance to the UK.

Access to space
The space above us gives people from other countries access to our own terrain. We have a direct interest in influencing the rights to and use of that access. We also have access to the space above the terrain of other countries, which in turn gives us opportunities and imposes obligations. These questions can be regulated only by international mechanisms. Power to influence the international regime depends in part on the extent of our own space assets.

Communications
Communications satellites now provide a normal means of transmitting information across national boundaries and round the globe. Those who are capable of building satellites and operate information services through them are in a privileged position to use them in pursuit of their own interests. This provides huge opportunities for those who hold these assets. Without such assets the scope for vulnerability is enormous. Britain has established a track record in this field, but the rapid pace of technological innovation and competition makes it difficult to maintain a comparative advantage without continued investment. These new communication links proffer the possibility of improving performance in many sectors of the economy and exercising a greater cultural and political influence elsewhere in the world. These opportunities are also being exploited by others, and are beginning to change the way in which the international political and economic system works.

Observation
Satellites provide the means for observing in now very fine detail what happens on the ground and in the oceans around the world. Knowledge derived from this growing bank of data will be increasingly relevant to the use of the Earth's resources, to assessments of the weather and environment and the deployment of military forces

(just to take a few illustrations). Access to that knowledge and the ability to interpret it confer economic and political influence. It is also directly relevant to the management of a country's security.

Science
Space provides the means to extend the frontiers of our knowledge about the planet which we inhabit and the cosmos beyond. Some of that knowledge – the science of space – feeds on our curiosity and has its own intrinsic value. But science in space is also now opening up the way for a far more sophisticated understanding of biology, the environment and materials. Research in many of these areas is still at an early stage but there are long-term prospects for applications in, for example, medicine, pollution control and the use of substances and materials for social and economic purposes. Public welfare and economic interest stand to benefit. People in an advanced country such as Britain have to choose how far they wish to be involved in the pioneering needed at the new frontiers of science and technology.

Security
The international security system is going through a process of potentially far-reaching change. Already the development of hardware and software for military systems makes space-derived data pertinent to a country's ability to deploy military power effectively and to monitor the parallel deployments of potential adversaries. Access to relevant space assets is especially important for those countries, including the UK, with nuclear capabilities. This raises immediately the question of whether it is better to rely on obtaining data from others, as an aid to targeting and assessments, or to strive for the relevant space assets independently. But space technology also impinges directly on the stability of the international security system. Efforts to reduce military tensions and arsenals can work only in so far as they can be implemented on a basis of careful monitoring and trust. Space systems provide valuable opportunities for monitoring new arms control and verification agreements.

Symbolism
Surrounding and beyond these specifics of space technology and the tasks which it may serve is a broader and less tangible dimension – namely the symbolism of a visible presence in space. If it is correct to

say that access to space confers economic, political and security influence, then it follows that some of this influence flows from a country being seen to be actively engaged in developing space capabilities. In many advanced countries this symbolism is viewed as being virtuous in its own right and therefore necessarily a vital asset. How large a range of space assets is needed to endow a country or group of countries with sufficient symbolic standing is a debatable and much debated question.

At one end of the spectrum engagement in a narrowly focused set of assets may be deemed sufficient. At the other end of the spectrum is the ownership of the full range of assets to the extent that virtual autonomy is achieved. Some policy-makers and advocates regard the ability to have their own people as well as machines operating in space as the critical threshold. It is around this threshold that much of the current European debate is focused. For Britain two questions then follow: what credence should be given to the symbolic attribute of space technology; and second, what kind of capability is needed to provide international influence. These arguments have not yet cut much ice in the British debate. They perhaps need much closer attention if in broader foreign policy terms Britain is to regain its standing as a major international actor.

The British record

Where then does Britain fit into this picture? British scientists and technologists were early into the field and some British policy-makers and industrialists were quick to recognize the potential utility to them of access to space technologies. British expertise in rocketry after the second world war partly accounts for this, but it was then complemented by an innovative scientific community along with a practical bent on the part of some service-providers and producer companies to look for useful applications of the techno-logical opportunities that emerged. This gave British programmes a more commercial orientation than was the case in some other European countries. But, and here the British approach diverged markedly from the French, space did not fire the collective British imagination. British space programmes emerged in an ad hoc and disjointed way, without either consistent public investment on a large scale or a sense that a country of the size and aspirations of the UK had to have a wide-ranging space policy. The British blew hot and cold about international collaboration, taking the apparently easy option on the military side of reliance on the close relationship (both political and scientific) with the US, and emerging in the European context as a somewhat hesitant partner.

The net result was that Britain retained a serious foothold in space, but both lacked a clear national strategy and depended on impulses from elsewhere (largely the US and ESA) to generate many of the new projects in which the British then participated. The foothold came to rest on the efforts behind the scenes of a relatively small group of scientists, technologists and industrialists, often operating through their own international networks and frequently working against the grain of the wider political and policy establishments. The lack of a powerful policy base and of a wider public constituency meant that publicly-funded space projects were always potential candidates for the axe in successive reappraisals of public subsidies. Those projects – both national and international – which survived did so often as a result of rearguard action by determined advocates. On the other hand, British space companies acquired considerably more self-reliance than some of their counterparts in other countries.

A new approach

By autumn 1985, however, the stage was set for a new act, in which Britain would emerge as a much more serious player. A new British National Space Centre (BNSC) would for the first time provide the basis for a national strategy. Scientists and technologists were involved in significant indigenous innovations which might give the UK a dynamic edge in the next generation of space projects. Hotol, the proposed new launch system under study by British Aerospace and Rolls-Royce, was a particular example. Equally important there were signs of increasing maturity in the markets for space technologies as existing and potential users began to appreciate that space offered them real assets. Thus the prospects for a more active national programme began to look bright.

At the same time new opportunities were opening up for international collaboration. The American proposal to create an 'international space station' invited European cooperation, within which a British-led polar platform might be developed. The member states of ESA were poised to endorse both this and several other projects in an ambitious and wide-ranging plan to achieve European autonomy in space. Britain was set to escape from its image abroad as a reluctant participant in international space programmes and to emerge instead as a committed and necessary partner. Yet by the summer of 1987 optimism had been replaced by despair. The BNSC had formulated its first strategic plan only to find that the government was not yet prepared to make available public funding on the scale required even to maintain established commitments, let alone to increase Britain's space capabilities. In the process Britain was beginning to emerge as the main dragger of feet in the negotiations about ESA's long-term plans. Understandably Roy Gibson, the first Director of the BNSC and a former Director-General of ESA, decided to resign. Simultaneously it was reported in the press that the Ministry of Defence would not after all proceed to develop the rumoured Project Zircon, a controversial proposal for an expensive British satellite to gather electronic intelligence.

The primary space industry in the UK therefore faced a daunting prospect. The first major contract by a British consortium for a Direct Broadcasting Satellite (DBS) had already been lost to Hughes, an American company. If the Europeans went ahead with their various and ambitious plans, but with only modest British participation, there would be limited scope for British companies to win a large stake in their development. If the British national programme was not to expand on either the military or the civilian side beyond projects already agreed, then the business generated nationally would be very limited. The scientific community which had played a key role over the years in maintaining an effective British foothold in space was vocally signalling its dismay at the outcome.

Disappointment and reappraisal

But does it matter? It is not the purpose of this paper to argue for a particular level of public investment in space or to plead for or against specific space projects. There are many other claims on the public R&D budgets, both military and civilian, and establishing a sensible hierarchy of priorities depends on finely balanced judgments about the feasible and the desirable. But it is the purpose of this paper to spell out the international implications of British policy

7

and to identify the international factors which decision-makers in the UK need to take into account, as they make their judgments about where space should figure in the rankings of claimants for public R&D funding and about which tasks can best be fulfilled by the exploitation of space technologies.

At one level decisions about the future of British space effort, in particular its volume of funding, rest on traditional and short-term calculations about just another area of technology where calls for public investment have to jostle with competing claims. In the current situation in the UK, with government policy firmly geared to reducing public subsidy and to encouraging a larger proportion of private investment, space may have little magical to offer, particularly against the counter-bids of technologies which appear to offer more rapid pay-offs. Add to this the inherited British resistance to 'mega-projects' with memories of Concorde still remarkably fresh in the collective, and especially the purse-holder's mind. Reckon too in the balance sheet a deep-rooted British caution, faced with the technological ambitions of many of their international partners. The critical sceptic can construct a powerful case. In such a context requests for larger-scale funding for space meet an instinctively austere response, bolstered by the fear that international collaboration as part of the package tends towards inherent inefficiencies, cost over-runs and a poor match between requirements and results. And the more dominant the financial considerations in the overall balance of assessment the more likely it is that the outcome will be parsimonious.

It is considerations of just this kind which appear to have predominated in the most recent appraisal of space policy by the British government. On 23 July 1987 Mrs Thatcher announced to the House of Commons that her government 'was not able to find any more resources' for the British space budget. Her statement and the surrounding briefings emphasized the financial dimension, the opportunity for private investors to support space and the absence of a rationale for switching resources from other areas of R&D to space. The words used gave little intimation that there were relevant ramifications for international policy, though the government's critics were quick to point out that there would be major repercussions in ESA and an impact on the American-inspired 'international space station'. Though the government announced a few weeks later that an extra £4 million would be made available to maintain temporarily ESA commitments to the Hermes and Columbus studies, this fell far short of the secure future sought by the space policy community. However, all was not lost since the government's wider review of R&D would look again at the space dossier and might yet produce a revised policy position.

The international dimension

It is the contention of this paper that the international dimension to British space policy is pervasive. It affects the shape of programmes, the competitiveness of the industry, relationships with partner countries, civilian services and military requirements.

Collaboration and dependence

Britain cannot mount a space programme independently of other countries. Exploiting space technology requires launch capabilities, payloads in orbit, appropriate facilities on the ground and a mix of human skills and ingenuity. The UK has at present no launch capabilities, produces only some kinds of relevant payloads and lacks the full ground infrastructure. Access to these other elements depends on their availability either by partnership arrangements or by purchase on commercial terms. Partnership arrangements require something from the UK in return on a basis of mutual interest and reciprocity. Purchase on commercial terms, for instance of launch facilities, means dependence on the supplier for both access and the terms of access – both price and conditions. In an area of technology where military and civilian technologies overlap conditions can be onerous. And in an area of technology where free market conditions do not apply, and will not apply for many years, prices are artificial and often determined as much by policy or political considerations as by simple economic criteria.

Collaboration also requires a consistency of commitment with partners in space as in any other area of military or civilian technology. There is now much evidence from areas other than space to demonstrate that those collaborative ventures which produce the best returns for the participants are those where habits of working together can become ingrained, trust achieved and a degree of predictability about partners' intentions established. Only under these conditions is there a real chance of ensuring that all of the partners' key requirements are satisfied and that the overall outcome is mutually beneficial.

Collaboration is also necessary to provide many satellite-based services which depend on global or regional organization. Three examples will serve to illustrate this. Communications links by satellite for telephone, telex and television among countries clearly require international regulation and management. Internationally these are handled within a framework set by the International Telecommunications Union, with services operated globally by Intelsat and within Europe by Eutelsat. In both organizations British Telecom International is the designated signatory, operating on public policy criteria before privatization, but subsequently more commercially and with a degree of competition with Mercury to provide UK services. Inmarsat, the recently established organization to handle maritime communications by satellite, is based in London and the UK is a very active member. Weather forecasting by satellite, seen daily on British television screens, is based on data from European satellites, now managed by Eumetsat, as well as from other sources.

Competitiveness
The primary space industry is not yet fully mature and it has to contend with competing technologies. Lead times are long, commercial returns are often speculative, markets are only just being defined and in all countries investment has been public-sector-led. Only in the ground segment is there anything like a 'normal' market in operation, and it is here incidentally that the Japanese industry has scored high in global exports, including penetration of the British domestic market. For the rest, on both the supply and the demand side, the terms have been set by decisions of public procurement to serve public policy goals. No national space company in Europe can operate on its own; all have consortia agreements with others, usually a mix of American and European companies. Only in France are the volume of business and the producer range large enough to sustain anything approaching a competitive business position, and even that statement deserves some qualification. Only in parts of the telecommunications sector is there an established industry with relatively mature technologies and able to finance directly the necessary investments. This does not altogether help, though, since the markets in many countries are tied

to public procurement. European markets for space technology remain much less developed than, for instance, the US domestic market, where the relative competitiveness of the American space industry is much helped by the volume of work for military projects. Thus in Britain, as elsewhere in Europe, many of the characteristics of an infant industry typify the space sector. To attain competitiveness for the primary producers and the suppliers of subsystems and components presents a real challenge. It means that purchasers, in choosing between competing tenders for space facilities and space systems, have generally to compare chalk and cheese, that is, typically, an American-led tender, based on an identifiable track record and seductive terms, and a European tender, based on a more individual proposal and sometimes on apparently less generous terms. Commercial judgments by purchasers will, of course, instinctively lean towards the immediately attractive package. But this further impedes the scope for the European supplier to develop its competitive position in an industry which has initially high R&D investment costs. For the European industry in general, and the British in particular, to cut through this vicious circle is not easy, though sometimes more possible for highly specialized companies operating in niche markets.

Since some markets are not developed, purchasers too are often inexperienced, inevitably so with new services such as DBS, or preoccupied with their own requirements, sometimes narrowly defined. Over-specification, parochialism and entrenched habits can all lead the purchaser to impose onerous conditions on the supplier, who then finds it harder simultaneously to compete for sales opportunities elsewhere.

Technology linkage and innovation
The space sector may appear highly specialized and idiosyncratic and to an extent of course it is. But it has three characteristics which link it to many other areas of technology. First, it is virtually impossible to disentangle civilian and military technologies and their application. To take one illustration, images from Earth observation satellites are used for both civilian and military purposes using similar, or even the same, satellites, ground stations and data processing equipment. It is just that where the use is military extra refinements will be needed, which might not be justified on purely

commercial grounds.

Second, the effective use of space depends on advances in many other areas of technology – materials, electronics, artificial intelligence and so on. The space sector has an important role in promoting developments as well as applying their results. In many of these areas Britain is engaged in international collaboration, through a mix of civilian programmes (European Community, Eureka, etc.) and military projects (such as the European Fighter Aircraft). Policy-makers have to decide whether to handle these as interdependent programmes and whether it is important for the UK to have the full range of relevant technological assets.

Third, a crucial feature of space technology is that it requires the integration and management of complex systems. It is no coincidence that the Japanese have identified space technology as a key route to enhancing their capabilites in systems integration and advanced software. It is precisely because of the complexity of space systems and their rigorous requirements that they depend on sophisticated assembly and management by highly skilled people. Once acquired the techniques and know-how of systems management can be turned to good use in other areas and indeed already are within the aerospace and electronics companies which currently produce so much of the hardware and software for space systems and sub-systems. One of the features of the proposed Hotol project is that it calls on a wide range of technological innovations and systems integration, some of which could be applied elsewhere.

For all these reasons the space sector has a particularly important role to play in technological innovation, with the corollary economic benefits which may then flow. The benefits and spin-offs will not necessarily emerge directly within the space sector. They may be applied elsewhere in the same company. Most of the primary space industry in Britain, as elsewhere, is actually attached to aerospace or electronics companies, usually with major roles as defence contractors. The extent to which technological diffusion takes place or a sufficiently highly skilled labour force is created will bear on industrial performance vis-à-vis other countries and on national workshares in international projects.

Security considerations
Three key developments in the field of security impinge on decisions about space applications for military purposes. First, the evolution

of the transatlantic defence relationship and the debate about a large role for collective West European activities set the context within which all British defence policy and procurement decisions are now made. The inherited British reliance on the American link for space-based systems may no longer adequately cover British defence requirements. Second, we have moved into a new generation of military systems in which space-based systems have become much more important. The American Strategic Defense Initiative is the clearest illustration, but less esoterically satellites for communications, intelligence gathering and reconnaissance are now a normal part of the hardware used to support military efforts. They are of special relevance to countries such as Britain with nuclear capabilities, where satellite-derived data are crucial for early warning about the intentions of others and for the credible deployment of nuclear weapons systems. These points are all relevant, irrespective of the question as to whether the American Strategic Defense Initiative is a desirable extension of military space activities. The third factor, mundane but crucial, is that all countries, including the UK, have over-stretched defence budgets. This makes decisions about priorities particularly difficult and opportunities for collaboration to share the burdens all the more important. But funding constraints also make the managers of defence budgets reluctant to take on extra costs of the R&D for all those space technologies which might possibly be relevant.

Preferred partners

If the arguments above are correct in highlighting these issues of international interdependence as directly relevant to decisions about space, it follows that they raise important questions about which partnerships should be most actively pursued. The British government has for many years concentrated civilian space expenditure on ESA programmes, with 80–85 per cent of the total now spent through ESA. The remaining national expenditure has remained constant and thus by comparison is small. This all stemmed from a view that for a modest spender it made most sense to lock into ESA enough to get a 'fair return' from the mandatory and the applications programmes, from which would flow a reasonable share of contracts for British industries and laboratories. Thus any British decision about the volume and direction of expenditure directly touches Britain's profile in ESA, unless the British government were prepared to forgo the residual national programme. Though ESA operates to an extent independently of other European fora, companies such as British Aerospace or Marconi and the other space producers are involved in many other aspects of European and international collaboration, so there are indirect consequences for them in other areas of changes in British space policy. Also, British attitudes to European space collaboration do feed into other countries' assessments of Britain as a partner.

The defence position is different. Britain uses national space-based systems for military purposes, mostly focused on the Skynet system of communications satellites. These are partly derived from American satellites and the system is interoperable with American systems and those of Nato, in which the British participate. In addition the British enjoy privileged access to US-sourced satellite data. There may be arguments for developing collective European space systems for various security purposes. But for the British to accept this would need a reappraisal of requirements and resources well beyond the exploratory discussions held so far with other European partners.

The British space programme is on all of these grounds set within the parameters of international policy. The bulk of the projects already completed or under development depend on international partnerships. The provision of services using satellites is largely orchestrated by international consortia, in which British companies participate as the suppliers of space systems or the providers of services. It was firmly in this context that the British National Space Centre in autumn 1985 set about drafting its new strategic plan. The interim announcement of July 1987 not to increase British expenditure on space risked foreclosing the options for intensifying collaboration just at the moment when proposals for the next generation of international space projects – both European and transatlantic – were ripe for decision. In the rest of this paper we explore the background to British policy against a backcloth of this crucially important international dimension and then identify the options and implications of recent and likely future developments. Central to the whole debate is the issue of which British interests are at stake in the choices of space policy objectives. Only on the basis of a decision about those interests can a sensible judgment be reached about where the critical threshold of involvement and investment should lie.

2

THE BRITISH RECORD

To be a major space power requires a large and sustained investment of skills, resources and technology. Space systems depend on three components: launchers; payloads in orbit; and a ground infrastructure to control missions and to process the data received. Only with all three can a country or group of countries aspire to autonomy in space. Nor will the investment be repaid unless there are enough customers available. In spite of being amongst the early pioneers of space technology Britain has never had a policy geared to autonomy. After early and unhappy experiences with launcher projects, British policy became much more selective. Britain acquired some real strengths in particular areas of space science and technology and an impressive track record in applying these to the production and utilization of space systems for certain purposes, especially in the field of communications, and more recently remote sensing. There is a sophisticated industrial base, which has been consolidated over the years in the main areas of specialization. But for the rest British space programmes have had to rely on facilities and capabilities elsewhere.

A historical perspective
To set the current pattern in context requires some understanding of how British policy and programmes have evolved. Britain was amongst the first group of countries to pioneer space systems, largely because the sophisticated rocket technology under develop-

15

ment to launch missiles provided a basis for space launchers. But when the Blue Streak rocket was deemed unsuitable as a delivery system for missiles, the British government investigated its development for space. Because the R&D costs would be high, Britain turned to its European partners with a proposal to 'Europeanize' Blue Streak. From this initiative ELDO was born, almost simultaneously with ESRO, the original European organization for space research.

But Britain quickly drew back from ELDO. The organization was judged by the British government to be incapable of building the planned Europa launch system out of the three separate stages to be provided by Britain, France and Germany. The judgment was reached in spite of the fact that the first stage of Europa, derived from Blue Streak, had scored a hundred per cent success in the twelve test launches. Britain then toyed with plans for an alternative and solely British launcher in the form of Black Arrow. But with the cancellation of this second project Britain withdrew entirely from the production of launch systems, though some British companies have since supplied sub-systems and components for Ariane.

This now fairly ancient history had a deep effect on what followed. The British thereafter looked to the United States for launch services. Their confidence in European collaboration had been badly dented, thus partly explaining subsequent British scepticism about Ariane. Perversely, however, the bad experience of ELDO proved a salutary lesson to its other members. ELDO was scrapped, but the launch programme subsequently adopted by ESA, christened Ariane and developed from French technology was managed much more tightly and coherently than the earlier Europa programme. These developments all took place at a time when Britain had been experimenting with other large projects in high technology, most spectacularly Concorde. But this was widely viewed in Britain as an expensive and non-commercial venture in which balanced collaboration with France appeared to be elusive.

On the other hand Britain was a much happier member of ESRO. There was a depth of expertise and enthusiasm in space science in the UK. Amongst the earliest satellites constructed in Britain was the Ariel scientific series, primarily designed for ionospheric measurements and X-ray astronomy. This in turn helped the then new space producer industry to develop skills which were to stand it in good stead as the opportunities began to emerge in other areas of space technology. Indeed this led the British to support ESRO's plans to develop applications as well as scientific satellites. This was a programme for which the British government had to argue hard in the early seventies at the point where successive European Space Conferences were deliberating the foundations and objectives of what became eventually the European Space Agency (ESA).

A selective approach

The British continued to investigate and invest in the space and ground segments, but still held back from heavy involvement in the development of launch systems. The path followed was gradualist and incremental. Programmes and projects were examined on their individual merits. Scientists, technologists and industrialists had to be determined and persuasive to win resources and contracts. In the process some areas of specialization began to emerge, subsequently to be welcomed as the basis of a more targeted approach. These included areas of space science, the development of communications satellites, for both civilian and military purposes, and some niche markets in sub-systems, components and software for space systems. An emerging capability in remote sensing was added later. This repertoire excluded as primary several items that appear in the more comprehensive programmes of some other countries, notably applied space science and manned flight. Some British scientists and companies, however, became involved in international consortia in some of these areas.

Specialization of this kind appeared sensible given the modest resources available from public and private investors. It had the advantage of positioning the British to make a mark internationally in the areas of strength, in terms of R&D contracts within the ESA framework and some access to international markets. But the lack of expertise and infrastructure in the neglected areas was to some extent self-reinforcing. It is of course often possible to make a late entry into a particular area of technology, but in space this really does depend on public investment in so far as new areas are by definition still some way from commercial viability. Nor is the British market for space systems, in either the private or the public sector, anything like large enough on its own to keep the industry's order-books full.

17

One other important consequence of the past was that as long as Britain chose to be a member of ESA and to keep the level of overall public investment modest, it followed that the purely national programmes were relatively small. A minimum level of commitment to ESA is required to win substantive as well as symbolic access to ESA programmes. British contributions have hovered not far above this minimum level, but they have nonetheless consumed a growing proportion of British public expenditure on civilian activities in space. Public investment is, of course, not the whole story, since the overall national investment in space, direct and indirect, is much larger. But public money and the policy goals on which it rests play a crucial role in trail-blazing and in providing a degree of longer-term security for the industrial and scientific communities.

How Britain compares
The comparisons conventionally shown put Britain in about third or fourth place on the space league table within Western Europe. This ranking reflects public budgets, industrial and scientific involvement and the range of activities. (Table 5.)

Budgets
Financial outlays provide one important measure of British involvement. The most accessible figures (Table 1) are those on public civilian expenditure. These show a rise in British expenditure broadly in line with the increase in ESA activities over the last decade or so, with the national programme having grown very much more slowly. Current allocations of expenditure continue to be heavily influenced by ESA activities. Their distribution among programme areas reveals as priorities: communications, Earth observation and science. (Table 2.) Aggregated with the declared figure of about £100 million for MOD expenditure, overall public expenditure is somewhat over £200 million. Table 3 gives British expenditure levels in comparison with those of several other countries. However, the comparison is partial in that military expenditure is not included either for the UK or for countries other than the USA and USSR. Countries such as Germany and Japan have no expenditure directly for military purposes.

But public spending tells only part of the story. The British space producer industry has an annual turnover of some £300 million.

British Telecom International has an investment of some £300 million in space-related facilities, both as a direct operator of services and as the designated British signatory of Intelsat, Inmarsat and Eutelsat. The industry as a whole probably spends about £100 million a year on the research and development of space systems, their infrastructure and their applications. It is much harder to gauge the extent of secondary financial activity in the UK. No good figures are available on the extent of private sector investment by the users of space technology, either by direct contracts for space systems or through the purchase of space-derived facilities. As a result almost all of the aggregate figures underestimate the total financial outlay within the UK and within that the level of private sector investment. All the same public expenditure has been a very important component as the primary source of R&D funding, especially to develop and prove technologies, as well as more obviously to promote scientific research. The reason for this is that so far most satellites have been commissioned for public markets. Only so far in the communications sector are there private as well as public customers.

National priorities
Science and communications have for nearly twenty years been the leading sectors of involvement. This is reflected in both the British emphases within ESA and the national programme to date (Table 4). These priorities have accounted in the past for well over half of the total civilian expenditure and almost all the military expenditure. As a result they have together dominated the efforts of the British space industry. One result of this, a considerable achievement, is that the British industry now has the largest capability in the world after the American in space communications. Thus British producers have won the tender for the next series of Nato communications satellites and scored some successes in contracts for Intelsat and Inmarsat. Another result is that British scientists, engineers and companies have established expertise and production capabilities in the ground segment, again largely to support communications systems.

More recently Earth observation has attracted increasing interest, a reorientation now evident in current allocations of public expenditure. (Table 2.) This goes towards both the production capability, mostly geared to ESA programmes, and the provision of facilities for processing data, the development of relevant satellite instrumentation and the quest for practical applications. These efforts are directed by the National Remote Sensing Centre. Interest in military applications of remote sensing is not yet expressed in national programmes. Britain has relied heavily on indirect access to US-gathered reconnaissance data, though the Canadian-led Radar-sat study has attracted British attention for both security and civilian purposes.

These priorities together consume over three-quarters of public civilian expenditure, much more if military expenditure is included. The remaining effort is spread rather thinly across the remaining range of space activities. One signal and deliberate omission is manned space flight. This has not so far emerged as a potential area of British expansion. Amongst the other Europeans the French have had astronauts on both Soviet and Nasa/ESA missions. The Germans have been vigorously interested, hence their key role in Spacelab and keen interest in the Ariane 5/Hermes combination and eventually the international space station. Of the smaller European countries the Dutch have shown interest sufficient to win a place for a Dutchman as an ESA astronaut on a Spacelab mission. The closest a British national has come to spaceflight was a place in the Shuttle mission which should also have launched a Skynet satellite in 1986, a mission displaced by the Challenger accident.

The other strikingly low priority since Britain withdrew from ELDO is launchers. British governments took the view that what mattered was access to launch services, for which a combination of good relations with the USA and eventually a small stake in Ariane were deemed to be a sufficient investment. More recently, however, interest has been rekindled by the potential of Hotol, the novel proposal for a revolutionary air-breathing engine which could power a fully reusable hypersonic launcher. DTI has contributed to the proof of concept study alongside British Aerospace and Rolls-Royce, the two companies engaged in the investigation.

If the Hotol study could successfully prove the viability of the basic design, it would have several important implications. First, it could bring Britain seriously back into the launcher business with a design to succeed the conventional rocket technology of Ariane for routine and flexibly sited launches. Secondly, however, it would require an international consortium to turn the concept into a development project and eventually production. The obvious choice of partners lies in Europe, hence the recent efforts to interest ESA. But it should be noted that other designs for 'space planes' are under urgent investigation. Thirdly, Hotol can be made to work only if it can draw on advances in several other areas of technology – materials, avionics, artificial intelligence and such like.

The industry
Generally the space industry has been narrowly construed to include the primary producers of space systems, sub-systems and specialized components. This categorization, however, seriously understates the level of industrial involvement in British space activities. Nonetheless the primary producers provide the industrial core relevant to Britain's basic space capability. Table 6 identifies the main companies and their product ranges.

Four points deserve emphasis. First, all the companies draw from and feed into parallel work in other sectors, often within the same company. For example, British Aerospace's space and communications division draws on skills and know-how from other parts of BAe. Secondly, all contracts require a consortium of several companies to provide in combination the necessary elements, though even then some components have to be brought in from outside the UK. Thirdly, companies, except for those in the ground sector, have to align themselves with partners from outside the UK. Table 8 summarizes one set of European consortia, established for ESA's science programmes. But these are complemented by many other consortia arrangements, some recurrent and some contract-specific, with both European and American industrial partners. Tables 9 and 10 illustrate these. Fourthly, the industrial partnerships cannot avoid issues of public policy, both because so many contracts are through public procurement and because producer companies in other countries mostly enjoy very close relationships with government.

The primary industry is on the face of it a relatively small employer. Precise figures are not available, but 3,500 employed is the generally cited figure. It is a misleading figure for several reasons. First, the main companies draw heavily on skills and expertise elsewhere in their labour forces to produce space systems. Secondly, the studies completed and products manufactured have a high added value achieved by small and expert teams. Thirdly, the industry works through a complex mix of prime contractors with subcontractors for sub-systems and components. The overall relevance and efficiency of the sector has to be judged in terms relevant to the character of the international consortia in which British companies take part.

It is even harder to gauge the economic relevance of the secondary industry. BTI, for example, employs some 1,000 people on space-related activities, a significant labour force in an important industry which uses space technology extensively. But for BTI, as for the other industries applying space technologies, space simply provides one means along with others for achieving their commercial and industrial objectives. For these reasons no agreed figures exist to indicate the size of the secondary industry or its industrial efficiency in terms of space as such.

One important attribute of the British industry – both primary and secondary – distinguishes it from most of its other West European counterparts. It has had to learn to survive in a much tougher environment and to acquire greater market awareness. Companies also stand at a greater distance from government than in other European countries. Liberalization of both the old PTT monopoly and market conditions more generally has gone much further than on the continent, though less far than in the United States.

This brief survey of Britain's national base in space technology serves to set the scene for the subsequent chapters on international collaboration and the development of policy. Little has been said about space science, in spite of its recurring importance in British and international space activities. But the heart of the debate about future British policy concerns the development and exploitation of space technologies.

3

BRITAIN AS AN INTERNATIONAL PARTNER

The British space programme is almost wholly locked into partnership arrangements with other countries at the levels of government, industry and science. Many of the British successes which have been scored in the exploration and exploitation of space have been the result of collaborative ventures nurtured over long periods. As has been argued earlier in this paper, without international collaboration British efforts in space would have been very modest. This is not to deny the importance or value of the purely national projects. Some have been crucial in developing spearheads of scientific research, technological innovation and industrial achievement. But the international dimension has been a necessary condition of consolidation and expansion. The only alternative way of acquiring a range of space assets would have been a much larger national investment and so far successive British governments have eschewed such a policy.

Yet Britain's reputation as a partner in space, especially in Europe, has often been seen as hesitant and half-hearted. This results mainly from three factors: first, the relatively small scale of the British national programme by comparison with some European counterparts; second, the troubled record of ELDO from which the UK withdrew; and third, a persistent British disinclination at the level of government to become heavily involved in the more ambitious collaborative projects. Instead British efforts have been heavily concentrated in the more immediately practical areas of collaboration, especially in communications satellites with the associated ground segment, and in some of the scientific projects with more readily demonstrable returns. Nor since the eventually aborted initiative to create ELDO has the UK been the source of grand new designs for space collaboration. The British have not sought to play in any sense a leadership role in Europe or to jostle for parity with the other major space powers in Europe. The continuing importance of the link with the United States in the use of space technologies for security purposes has added to an impression of British detachment from the collective European enterprise in space.

The consequences of this pervasive international engagement combined with a cautious policy stance in the UK have been fourfold. First, Britain has been rather dependent on international initiatives to stimulate interest in new projects. Dependence in the US-UK context has had the added element of asymmetry: the link is necessary for the UK, but not for the US. Secondly, British influence on international collaboration has been limited. In the European context British influence is substantially less weighty than French, an obvious point, but also perhaps now than German or latterly Italian. Thirdly, no clear profile of the overall British space effort can be identified separately from the collaborative projects through which most of it is channelled. And in the absence of a space strategy British participation in international collaboration has depended on rather segmented decisions about individual projects, each on its separate merits. Again there is a clear contrast with several other European countries, not only France, Germany and Italy, but countries such as Sweden, where there has been a more sharply defined approach, and even some of the much smaller European countries which have concentrated on specialized niches. But fourthly, though the practice of British space policy is international, individual points of decision have been addressed from a rather parochial national perspective.

The European arena

The lion's share of British public expenditure on civilian space is spent through ESA programmes with their R&D emphasis. In terms of a formal description of Britain's European involvement ESA thus occupies a central position. But this is actually only part of a larger, much less well-appreciated picture. British agencies or companies are deeply involved in the provision of European services through space, most obviously through Eutelsat, for telecommunications, and Eumetsat, for weather forecasting data. British producer companies are deeply immersed in European consortia, both the larger companies with a central interest in space, British Aerospace and GEC-Marconi, and other companies with space interests, Ferranti, Logica, Thorn-EMI and so on. In addition the increasing interest in space technologies now being articulated in the European Community directly involves the UK.

Two elements are strikingly absent from Britain's European repertoire. One is the relative lack of involvement in new projects involving only two or three European countries at the level of public policy. There are several cases of Franco-German projects, but no Franco-British, though Rosat (an X-ray astronomy satellite) is being developed by British and German companies, and Iras (an infra-red astronomy satellite) has been a partnership of the UK and the Netherlands with Nasa. The French have looked for and found partners on some projects which fell outside ESA, notably the Belgians and Swedes in the Spot programme of civilian reconnaissance satellites. There is as yet no comparable British-led initiative. The other missing element is on the defence side. British governments have so far been sufficiently satisfied with the combination of US-UK links and shared Nato systems not to look more than tentatively to other Europeans for collaborative arrangements. This again contrasts with the French, now engaged, for example, in developing Helios, a military reconnaissance satellite with some Italian and possible Spanish participation. The fact that France is not part of the integrated military structure of Nato partly, but only partly, explains the contrast.

The European Space Agency

ESA continues thus far to be the predominant European framework for collaboration. In spite of British disappointment at the outcome of ELDO and helped by more positive experience in ESRO, the UK was a founder member of ESA and has retained a commitment to it. Britain makes its GNP-linked contribution to the mandatory programmes of ESA, for which in return come a guaranteed place in ESA decision-making and a pro rata return to British industry and to the scientific community. Britain has also participated actively in many of the applications programmes. The initial decision to make this pledge to ESA at its inception was not easily reached in the early seventies. But the Ministry of Aviation Supply, then led by Michael Heseltine, eventually won the argument within the Conservative government of Mr Heath. Subsequent British policy has been designed to make a positive virtue out of that rather finely balanced decision. In the mid-seventies a 'package deal' was struck among the governments of ESA, which has largely governed the subsequent emphases of member states' policies within ESA. Britain's stake in the package turned out to focus on the applications programme for telecommunications and to a lesser extent remote sensing, alongside a continuing share of scientific work following on from ESRO.

Mandatory programmes
There are many examples of projects and missions carried out within the mandatory programmes of ESA, in which British involvement has been significant and satisfaction evident. Amongst the range of scientific programmes of ESA the British have established special strengths. The scientific missions have included the GEOS programme (for investigating particles and fields in the magnetosphere) and the Giotto mission of 1985 to intercept Halley's comet. British Aerospace was prime contractor for both. British companies have provided sub-systems for many other scientific missions, such as Hipparcos (measuring star motion), Exosat (identifying X-ray sources), IUE (ultra-violet explorer with Nasa) and ISEE (for magnetospheric research). They have also contributed to the ESA elements of the Spacelab and the Space Telescope. British laboratories and universities have also been closely involved in these and other missions, largely under the aegis of the Science and Engineering Research Council.

Optional programmes
These have fallen into two main categories: the technology-proving applications programmes; and the special projects, such as the Ariane launchers. ESA members choose on an à la carte basis whether to participate in the optional programmes and for what financial stake. Only those ESA members which opt in take part in subsequent decision-making on each venture. On the applications side the preponderant involvement of the UK has been in the communications projects sponsored by ESA. British Aerospace has been the prime contractor for OTS (an experimental orbital test

satellite to prove new technologies and their derivatives); Marecs (for maritime communications and now leased to Inmarsat); the European Communications Satellites (for trunk telecommunications and now operated by Eutelsat); and Olympus (originally L-Sat designed to prove follow-on technologies for conventional telecommunications, business services and TV broadcasting). In all of these Marconi Space Systems has also been a significant provider of subsystems.

This considerable specialization reflects a developing preference by both government and industry in the UK to give primacy to applications of space technology where the customers or potential customers could be relatively clearly identified (whether private or public purchasers) and where the markets were ripe for commercial exploitation. This has had the added advantage of helping British companies to tender credibly and successfully at an international level, as well as to develop an expanding market for satellite-based telecommunications in the UK. The manufacturing strengths are to be found in the design and production of satellites, sub-systems and the ground segment. In this field there are sophisticated British producers and purchasers.

The British have played a less prominent role in the other ESA applications programmes, such as Meteosat (a weather satellite series) or ERS (for remote sensing). This skewed involvement reflects two different factors. First, British companies could not have expected to be prime contractors across the range of ESA programmes. Indeed the fair returns (or *juste retour*) policy of ESA is designed expressly to prevent the big contractor or country from sweeping the board. Nonetheless British companies have provided sub-systems for Meteosat and ERS. But there have also been less indigenous depth in remote sensing and less well-defined markets than in telecommunications, a position which is now changing, with the development of the National Remote Sensing Centre. It is also important to note that British companies have provided, often as prime contractors, ground equipment for ESA programmes across the range of communications, remote-sensing and scientific activities.

The picture as regards the other projects of ESA has been quite different. These are generally expensive, ambitious and deliberately innovative. They have included the original Ariane launcher programme, the current Ariane 5 and Hermes studies, ESA's first

27

venture into manned flight through Spacelab and the proposed ESA elements of the 'international space station' initiated by the United States. So far the British government has played only a very modest role in this range of projects at the development stages and thus won only a small part in the contracting consortia. So, for example, Britain initially did not join the Ariane programme and when it eventually joined did so with a low financial stake, 3.73 per cent. A similar approach characterized Britain's initial response to the Hermes study. In contrast interest in the space station has been more enthusiastic, hence the inclusion of the polar orbiting platform under potential British leadership as one of the ESA elements in the space station project.

This limited contribution has secured British involvement in the relevant follow-on decisions, but it has not so far endowed Britain with a large influence on the designs of the projects or the subsequent steps to make them operational. The consequences have been twofold. First, Britain has not been viewed by its European partners as a deeply committed participant. Secondly, these big individual projects (as compared with the valuable but more mundane communications programmes) have had far less impact on British opinion than say the launch programme in France or the manned flight programme in Germany. Thus while the British stance reflected a conscious emphasis, it also contributed to the low profile of space activities within the UK.

This is all highly pertinent to the current debate within ESA about the next generation of ESA projects. The Ariane 5/Hermes combination together with the ESA contribution through the Columbus programme to the 'international space station' are likely to consume a very large proportion of ESA resources, if they go ahead broadly as proposed. This may limit resources available for other programmes. The space industry in the UK needs to win orders to take it through the next decade and beyond, given that lead times are long and for some parts of the space business the customers are few in number. This raises important questions about what Britain would want from the new ESA package deal, which has yet to be definitely struck. This explains British insistence on a polar platform, which would be British-led, as a necessary facet of the Columbus programme. This is not to deny the importance of other British industrial contributions to big ESA projects, such as Ferranti's manufacture of guidance systems for Ariane or Logica's provision of software and systems expertise.

The British position could change dramatically if there were a British-initiated project on the ESA list of major new programmes. Here Hotol takes on a significance which goes far beyond the study's basic aim of developing an advanced and reusable launch vehicle in Europe. Hotol is too large a project for the UK to develop on its own. Collaborating partners are necessary and the industry's preference is for a European consortium to complement and supplement Ariane in the next century. The Hotol idea obviously has to stand or fall on its technology and engineering, currently under appraisal. But if proved and 'Europeanized', it could enhance British influence and industrial returns within ESA.

A balance sheet
Britain has been a serious member of ESA. It has contributed to and gained from the mandatory programmes in the chosen fields of specialization. The choice of Roy Gibson to head BNSC also served to enhance British influence. However, ESA is essentially a research and development organization and the closer communications satellites come to real market profitability the less will fall to ESA as distinct from to the operating agencies or markets. Pressures on the ESA budget may well also mean that there will be limited scope for expansion of the scientific projects which have been of real interest to the UK. The fair returns policy of ESA has been some guarantee of returns and Britain has so far won back a positive industrial return. But it has to be recognized that all ESA members are pushing to maximize their own returns.

It would require a strategic decision on the part of the UK to claim and pledge a larger stake. Given the character of many of the optional programmes this would also require a long-term commitment from the British to support innovative projects, the commercial returns for which are by definition speculative. Hotol, for instance, could not become an ESA programme unless British commitment were solid. And in turn this would raise the issue of whether Britain should or could claim the role of project leader, in itself a novelty outside the communications sector.

Beyond this lie the questions of how important the UK judges the overall shape of ESA's long-term plan and how proactive British policy should be. ESA has set itself the goal of achieving European autonomy in space. Though endorsed in outline by the British government at the ESA ministerial meeting in 1985 and indeed greeted with some enthusiasm at the time by Geoffrey Pattie, then the responsible minister, the goal has attracted rather more determined support from British industry. The reason for this is fairly plain. An ambitious European programme, if successfully achieved, would, in the view of the industry, generate contracts, attract user and wider public interest and contribute to Europe's ability to compete in tough international markets. The success of ESA's long-term programme obviously depends in part on the intrinsic features of the particular projects, their technological content and feasibility. But it also depends on how far different national and industrial requirements can be met and on whether mutually satisfactory arrangements can be made on the basis of accepted reciprocities. At this stage it is not evident that British policy takes full account of these preconditions. And without that the new ESA package may not emerge in a form which meets British interests.

The European Community
The EC has recently begun to assert a role for itself in the field of space technology. This could include a contribution to technological innovation, most obviously in adjacent technologies such as advanced avionics, artificial intelligence, research into new structural materials, exotic energy sources and such like. There is also some scope for the EC to pioneer and promote applications of space technology, such as the use of Earth observation data for crop forecasting or communications links across Europe, including the less accessible regions or mobile vehicles. The EC also makes enforceable legislation which shapes the regulatory framework for manufacturers, traders and the providers of services. This takes on an enhanced importance in the light of moves to establish a full internal market, targeted for 1992, against a backcloth of wider international pressures to liberalize markets. In addition the EC has an important role in negotiating on trade issues. Lastly, there is a potential role for the EC, or at least European Political Cooperation, in responding to changes in the context of European security and setting the context in which policies and programmes might then be developed.

Several of the R&D programmes of the EC touch on technologies relevant to space – some complementary and some alternatives. Esprit, Race, Brite and Star all have elements which are highly pertinent in terms of both their technical content and the methods used to stimulate scientific and industrial collaboration across national frontiers. The same is true to a lesser extent of the wider Eureka initiative which complements Community programmes on a wider European basis. Many British companies with space interests have become involved in these various initiatives and have been broadly content with their early results.

The British government has, however, cast an exceedingly critical eye over the R&D programmes of the EC and the levels of funding proposed. Indeed the result was to delay decisions on the Framework Programme for some months and to reduce the funding not only well below what was proposed by the Commission, but also below what many EC member states were prepared to accept. British arguments about the EC programmes closely resemble those deployed in the domestic debate over space policy, the need for prudence and frugality and the importance of stimulating a different balance between private and public investment. Interestingly the two sets of issues came to ministerial attention more or less simultaneously from autumn 1986 to spring 1987. That the attention proved so critical in both cases has contributed to a perception of the UK as a very reluctant partner in European technological collaboration. Whatever the rights and wrongs of the British assessments, there have been European political costs as a result of the way in which the arguments were deployed.

In sharp contrast the UK has been the most vigorous of supporters of the moves to achieve a single internal market within the EC. Here British doctrines coincide with declared EC objectives and extend to the related areas of wider liberalization of markets and procurement. Not only that but the British companies involved in the space sector are much more sympathetic to market opening than many of their counterparts in other European countries. The fact that telecommunications services in the UK are now provided by operators in the private sector with a degree of domestic competition further accentuates British interests in pioneering a more market-oriented approach across Europe. In this field both producers and operators in the UK draw heavily on American experience, whereby, they believe, early acceptance of an 'open skies' policy hastened the commercial viability of space-based services and stimulated market expansion. They also recognize the importance of Europeans positioning themselves to measure up to anticipated developments in American industry and public policy.

European security
The UK is heavily engaged in European collaboration in security across the spectrum from strategic policy to procurement and logistic rationalization. So far, however, this has barely touched the space segment beyond loosely based European discussions of the American Strategic Defense Initiative and rather tentative discussions with the French government. In communications the UK relies for global coverage on a combination of the national Skynet system and the Nato communications system, viewed by the British as both European and Atlantic in character. In most other fields the British have relied heavily on access to information from space-based systems through the connection with United States, discussed below. The British have not looked for other security projects in space in association with European partners.

This British approach has rested on an assessment of resources, requirements and collaborative opportunities which may now merit reappraisal. For reasons discussed earlier in this paper the context is changing and space-based systems have increased in relevance, but remain costly. Reconnaissance satellites are the most obvious candidates for attention as collective European ventures. There is a shared European interest in having its own sources of satellite reconnaissance data, for operational planning, crisis monitoring, and the verification of arms control agreements. This accounts for the discussions between France and Germany, not yet translated into an agreement, and the confirmed Italian and possible Spanish decisions to associate themselves with the French Helios Programme. But as these discussions have revealed it is hard in practice to define an agreed profile of common requirements.

All this adds up to a plausible rationale for the British not moving at this stage to increase space capabilities on either a national or a European basis, especially when it is by no means self-evident which collaborative framework in Europe might be appropriate and acceptable. As against this it must be recognized that the situation is moving fast between the USA and the USSR and that as it does the apparently easy complementarity of British and American security interests may diminish. A head of steam is beginning to build up in favour of a European security identity expressed in space as well as through other vehicles. Indeed the companion European volume to this paper argues vigorously for hastening in this direction. British policy makers may find themselves having to rethink their approach sooner rather than later.

Collaboration with the United States
British space programmes and the use by the British of space-derived data have both been much influenced by the transatlantic link. This has been most evident on the military side, but there have been also many links in terms of access to technology and industrial collaboration. Current attitudes to this transatlantic link display a mix of conflicting views. The space community in Britain has gained much and on the military side expects to continue to do. But there are nagging doubts about what lessons can be drawn from experience to date as well as about the prospects for the future. The experience of Spacelab induced European caution, reflected recently in the testing negotiations between Nasa and ESA about the terms of European participation in the American-proposed international space station.

Military links
These fall into three categories. First is the direct collaboration out of which British space systems have been developed. The Skynet communications satellite owed much to earlier American R&D, though subsequent development has been in the hands of British contractors. It was logical and at the time financially attractive that Skynet should be capable of interoperability with Nato and US systems and that Shuttle should be the launcher, until the Challenger accident forced a switch to Ariane. A corollary was to have been a place for a British payload specialist on board a Shuttle flight. Though developed and deployed as a British system, Skynet in a very practical sense complements Nato's integrated system. This helped in 1987 to make credible, and eventually successful, the tender from British Aerospace and Marconi to supply the next generation of communication satellites for Nato from a derivative of Skynet. Had a project such as Zircon been agreed to provide a

national satellite for electronic intelligence, it too would have leant on American technology and expertise.

Secondly, there is a very longstanding agreement between the UK and the USA to share military intelligence. This sprang very naturally from the close military relationship between the two countries in the second world war and was equally logically complemented by similar arrangements with Australia, Canada and New Zealand. At the outset this had nothing at all to do with space. However, as space-based systems became an increasingly useful source of military intelligence, so they were swept into the same arrangements. It was not that the British government chose to establish a new agreement specifically related to space. But if the Americans were willing to extend the coverage of a prior agreement, there was little reason for the British to demur, especially since this obviated the need to develop an expensive and duplicating national system or to set about the difficult task of constructing an alternative arrangement with other partners. The utility of the link was demonstrated during the Falklands war, which reinforced the existing British satisfaction with the established exchanges of data, though it also revealed corollary constraints.

This remains the essence of the British position. There is little incentive to change that position as long as British military commanders and defence planners are persuaded that they have sufficient access to relevant intelligence which effectively costs them nothing, or as long as they believe that the American government is neither holding back crucially relevant material nor overlaying it with distorted interpretation. There is, however, a growing political problem in the European context. Other European governments do not enjoy the same privileged access to US data, though several have some access under more limited bilateral arrangements. British policy-makers have to recognize the irritation caused to their European partners and take care to demonstrate that their logical policy arrangements are not based on suspicions of fellow Europeans.

The third element relates to American-inspired initiatives and British reactions to them. SDI met with an ambivalent response in the UK. Deep scepticism about the merits and feasibility of SDI has spread wide, including within government. This has, however, been counterbalanced by the Prime Minister's concern to applaud President Reagan's determination to forge ahead with the programme of R&D. The government was also keen to ensure that British scientists and industrialists had access to prized contracts. It was for all of these reasons that the British government signed a Memorandum of Understanding with the American government. Contracts have subsequently been placed within the UK, though fewer than expected and the attached terms (about who has access to the fruit of the R&D) have given rise to criticism. It should however be stressed that the SDI debate within the UK has not been viewed as in essence about space policy.

Civilian collaboration and competition
It is tempting to extrapolate from the security relationship a contented bilateralism on a larger canvas. There is indeed some evidence to support this. British space companies are deeply immersed in collaboration with American companies, incidentally a comment that could be made of other European countries. British Aerospace does more work with Hughes, a leading American company, than it does for ESA contracts. British producers of space systems, again like their European counterparts, rely on some American-sourced components. Many British payloads have in the past been launched by Shuttle. There are bilateral links with Nasa in space science and technology.

Yet increasingly there are other factors to be weighed in the balance. First, British satellites have been launched by both Shuttle and Ariane and British companies welcome the competition between the two. But Shuttle's problems have forced the British to look again at the launch services currently available and the long-term prospects. This has heightened British interest in Ariane and alternative launchers, in the short term perhaps even the Soviet Proton, and in the longer term a European successor to Ariane. At one level this illustrates simply prudence on the part of industry to gain access to other launch services. But at another level it raises important foreign policy considerations. It would be illogical to ask the industry to be more competitive and then refuse permission to launch on a reliable and financially attractive Soviet launcher. It may not be long before the British government has to confront this question, quite likely in the face of American government pressures for refusal.

Secondly, American industry competes fiercely in international markets. Though this may well provide a spur to British companies to perform well, it also leads to some considerable concern. In the bidding for international tenders in Intelsat, for example, American and especially Californian companies have been outstandingly successful. European companies, including the British, have found it hard to win tenders. The American domestic market is not easy to penetrate. And the British market is open to penetration. The award of the first British DBS contract to Hughes rather than the consortium led by British Aerospace aptly illustrates this. Hughes, with its large resources but badly in need of orders, was able to offer terms which European manufacturers could not reasonably match and the British purchasers were under no countervailing pressure to buy British or European. This is the downside of a philosophy which advocates free competition. But as yet there is little undistorted competition in the space sector.

Thirdly, the fine line between military and civilian technologies in space makes it very hard in practice on the civilian side to escape American controls on technology transfers and exports of sensitive products. British companies express some concern that over-reliance on collaboration with the US could therefore carry real risks, unless there is counterbalancing action by the British government to protect them from American technology controls. There is, after all, an important foreign policy dimension to the development and deployment of space systems by British companies. This is also reflected in the negotiations with the US over the 'international space station', in which ESA has been at pains to ensure inter alia that American terms are not too onerous or restrictive on these issues of technology transfer.

The balance sheet
The transatlantic dimension is both an asset and a complication for the British space programme. On the security side persistent intimacy remains the dominant mode, particularly among senior military officers, and a powerful counterbalance to any arguments for seeking collaboration with European partners. On the civilian side the picture is much more blurred. British companies want to continue to choose industrial partners from both the United States and elsewhere in Europe, according to context. But they are increasingly looking to government to define a clearer position on the foreign policy dimensions to their commercial choices. And they recognize the value of being able to operate sometimes on a

collective European basis against the large power base and domestic market of the American industry.

Other partners
Britain's international links with other space powers beyond the USA and the rest of Europe are limited, though the British National Space Centre has been seeking to expand them. The British government has been examining with some interest the Canadian Radarsat. This would provide radar reconnaissance data, especially useful for gathering information over oceans relevant to both surface vessels and submarines. In the civilian field contacts have been established with the Soviet, Chinese and Indian space programmes. In 1986 Roy Gibson visited Moscow and reached agreement that British and Soviet scientists would collaborate on Phobos, an unmanned probe to Mars, as well as explore other possible areas of collaboration, such as those envisaged by the new Institute of Space Biomedicine at the University of Sheffield.

International regulation and management
The day-to-day work of the space business is set within parameters determined by international negotiation. Part of the broad framework flows from the UN and its Committee on the Peaceful Uses of Outer Space (Copuos). Frequencies for the transmissions made by satellites are determined within the International Telecommunications Union (ITU). British positions on the issues within these frameworks have to be articulated by government representatives on the basis of a definition of where British interests lie. Legal, commercial and financial transactions relevant to space are already circumscribed by international agreements and there are likely to be more rather than less negotiations amongst governments to define an international space regime. The international space station will similarly be governed by international rules as well as by agreement among the participating countries.

Satellite services operated across national boundaries require international management, for which the various satellite consortia have been established – most particularly Intelsat, Eutelsat and Inmarsat. Britain's designated signatory in these is British Telecom International, responsible for a capital subscription, service operation and the management of access to the satellite systems which the consortia operate. They are of special interest to the UK precisely because of British strengths in the communications field. But there are also some accidental comparative advantages. In communications services (as in air services) Britain remains a gateway to Europe. The modern satellite links have inherited a pattern established long ago by Cable and Wireless, indeed this accounts for the importance of the ground segment and size of markets for the British industry. This advantage has been reinforced by the position of English as the language of international communications.

The resulting commercial business for the UK is considerable, indeed this explains, in the new age of privatized services, the enthusiasm of Mercury for a share of the business. Hence there are clear British commercial interests – for both producers and service operators – at stake in this field. Maintaining a competitive edge internationally is crucial, but domestic competition is also now beginning to emerge. Because the satellite consortia include public agencies as signatories, if no longer so from the UK, negotiations within them cannot be confined to commercial and technical considerations. Nor can the terms of the relevant agreements be easily adjusted as the commercial context evolves. This leaves BTI with a dual task: to speak for the UK and to look for ways of consolidating its own business interests.

The implications
This survey should make fully evident just how important the international dimension is to everything which Britain does in space. Obviously the larger the British programme, the more important it is to develop a carefully orchestrated approach to the way in which British interests are promoted in international discussions of space issues. But it would be an illusion to think that these issues would cease to be relevant if Britain were to retain only a modest involvement in space. Developments in space technology will continue apace. Their exploitation for economic and security purposes will be pursued. The use of space technologies and the operation of space-based services will continue to expand in the UK and globally irrespective of formal government policy. British policy-makers will therefore have to continue to address the questions of what kind of relationships with other countries and what kind of international regimes to manage space are likely to be most appropriate.

4

IN SEARCH OF A STRATEGY

The decision of January 1985 to create the British National Space Centre in November 1985 marked a deliberate innovation in the management of British space policy. Prompted by the results of a high-level enquiry chaired by Sir Robin Nicholson, then the Chief Scientific Adviser to the government, it was intended to coordinate thoroughly and strategically government policy with a close involvement of industry and the scientific community. It was well recognized by those involved that this required a careful appraisal of the interconnections between British policy and the international collaborative context. Indeed the knowledge that ESA was scheduled to take a major round of decisions on its long-term plan during 1987 gave the BNSC a clear target at which to aim.

This chapter examines the intentions and the results of this initiative along with the processes through which the British participate in and influence decisions in international fora dealing with space activities. It also identifies those features of the wider policy process within the UK which shape the way in which space policy is formulated and implemented.

The background

Policy coordination
The British policy process is predicated on the principle of collective cabinet responsibility, unlike the processes in many other countries

where individual ministries have a greater degree of formal responsibility for the subjects within their statutory domain. In Britain, therefore, it should follow that the government determines policy only by drawing together the different dimensions relevant to any specific topic on the basis of inputs from those different departments (or ministries) which have relevant expertise or operational responsibilities. It is certainly the case that the British have a highly articulated system of inter-departmental coordination, generally managed by the Cabinet Office and its various secretariats and expressed through inter-departmental committees at both official and ministerial level. The results of this process should be that both the civilian and military dimensions of policy issues are taken into account and balanced; that informed decisions can be reached about priorities and relevant public expenditure; and that the complementary and competing interests of different departments can be appraised and manipulated to serve the overall interests of the UK, as determined at least by government.

Reality is of course often different. The mechanisms of central coordination can handle only a certain amount of business effectively and normally give most attention to those issues with current high salience. In the British context space policy issues have only occasionally been viewed as highly salient, in contrast to their treatment in France as persistently salient. Between the periods of salience, many policy areas including space policy have been left to the care and maintenance of the individual departments with operating roles and to the judgments of policy-makers within them as to when and whether inter-departmental consultations are necessary. Even when such consultations take place they do not necessarily produce a rounded strategic view. Much coordination is either information exchange, rather than sharp appraisal, or aimed at conflict avoidance rather than conflict resolution. The typical outturn is the 'pragmatism' so deeply ingrained in the British process, or the 'disjointed incrementalism' of the policy analyst.

The single policy mechanism which cuts across this recurrently is the annual determination of public expenditure levels and associated instruments for financial control. Thus the Treasury has always had a particularly strong position in inter-departmental coordination on any issue involving significant public expenditure. This often skews decision making to give primacy to financial arguments above assessments of substance, especially where large-scale projects are under review with their long lead times. The need to control overall levels of public expenditure and corollary long-term commitments has been a dominant influence since the mid-seventies, though it was by no means a new phenomenon. Blue Streak was cancelled as a British rocket project in 1959, when financial assessments tipped the balance of the defence arguments. Since the arrival in office of Mrs Thatcher's government in 1979, public expenditure decisions have been increasingly rigorous and the weight of the Treasury proportionately enhanced.

Departmentalism
The limits of central coordination mean that the approaches and behaviour of individual departments in practice exercise a crucial influence on policy outcomes. In the case of space policy the main responsibilities have rested with the Ministry of Defence (MOD) and on the civilian side the Department of Trade and Industry (DTI) and its precursors. Both are large departments with wide-ranging domains. Within both, space projects and space budgets have had to jostle with many competing claims for attention and funding. The parameters of decision-making on space have been set by other programmes, so that space assets were seen as relevant not in their own right but to the extent that they served other policy goals. In this sense space policy has been a dependent or subordinate area, never able to shape the terms of policy debate on other issues.

Both departments have found their budgets under increasing strain. Both have important sponsor-client relations on other projects with British Aerospace and GEC-Marconi (the two lead companies as satellite producers). Both, since 1979, have been subject to vigorous reviews of expenditure and priorities, a process not yet complete for either department. Moreover, though there are many areas of technological overlap between MOD and DTI it has often proved difficult for the two departments to sort out bilaterally the convergences and divergences of interest, as the Westlands helicopter case illustrated. In the space sector there is a particular difficulty. Prudence suggests that it is in Britain's security interests to retain the technology and production base from which space systems could subsequently be developed if needs must. But from an industrial perspective there is little to be said for keeping in mothballs expertise or capacity that may never be used.

Within the Ministry of Defence, circumstances have never allowed 'space' to be high on the agenda. Britain's transition from being a global power at the end of world war two to a medium sized European power in the 1980s has meant a constant battle to reconcile the declining resources for defence with security commitments that were shrinking less rapidly. Thus, the opportunity to move into new fields, particularly those that appeared to be less than essential to Britain's more modest role, were neither politically welcome, nor likely to receive serious consideration in the budgets of the three individual service departments as they struggled to maintain their existing programmes. It is notable that space policy has only once been even modestly addressed in any of the Defence White Papers of the last twenty-five years. That was in 1966, when a Sub-Committee of the Defence Committee reported on the military interest in space. The programme, outlined in four brief paragraphs, was principally in the field of research and was costed at £4 million in a total defence research and development budget of £275 million. The White Paper announced that the UK's major contribution to an experimental satellite communication system, in collaboration with the US Department of Defense, would be ground stations.

During the 1950s, the close association of the Royal Air Force with the US Air Force ensured that Britain kept a close eye on what the US were doing in this field. The requirement for manned aircraft to fly higher and faster took them to the lower regions of space, which was thus seen as a natural extension of the airman's environment. The development of unmanned long range rockets also fell conveniently within the Air Force's remit as an alternate means of delivering airborne weapons over long distances. Thus it was the RAF which bought from the US, and operated under a dual US/UK key system, the nuclear headed Thor missiles, which together with the V-bomber force comprised Britain's deterrent in the 1950s. The subsequent British decision to abandon Blue Streak and the American decision to abandon Skybolt removed from the RAF the principal responsibility for Britain's nuclear deterrent, which went to the Royal Navy. There was, however, little enthusiasm in naval circles for the decision to build four Polaris submarines, because it was feared that this ambitious programme could be successfully undertaken only at an unwelcome cost to the performance of other important naval tasks. The Polaris programme was, in the event, most successfully managed and completed. But the Navy had no ambitions for the wider role in space to which their dark blue brothers across the Atlantic seemed to be aspiring.

The Navy had traditionally assumed prime responsibility for the global network of wireless communications that linked, not only Her Majesty's Ships at sea worldwide, but also the outposts of Britain's empire. Satellite relay stations in space offered possibilities for a communications network of immensely improved performance. However, as the 1966 White Paper announced, research was also being undertaken on methods of communication not involving the use of man-made satellites, by use of 'moon bounce' or the use of 'space junk'. But the naval approach to space communications was that of the professional communicator and not that of the space specialist, an attitude reinforced by the priority being given in Britain's own programme to ground stations. There were very few space enthusiasts in the top echelons of the navy.

In the intelligence field Britain was well to the fore in the use of communications intelligence. The intercept and analysis of radio traffic and a sophisticated direction-finding network played a key role in the support of military operations, particularly at sea. Thus, the armed services were during the Second World War much involved in the tasks of gathering, analysing and disseminating intelligence. But as the war turned into an uneasy peace, the services were less involved in the collection of intelligence, and more concerned with its analysis and interpretation. Since the United States supplied a great deal of high grade intelligence to the UK under the agreements made at the end of the war, Britain was very slow to understand the revolution in methods of intelligence collection that was offered by advances of technology, particularly in space. The armed services were also slow to appreciate the opportunities that new technology offered for the tactical collection and use of intelligence. Without a single, separately funded and organized intelligence agency in Britain, and with the services 'cushioned' by the supply of raw data from the United States, there was no effective pressure from the intelligence community for Britain to expand its own space capabilities.

Thus, nowhere in the British defence establishment were any effective champions of space to be found. Space was something which might be useful for facilitating certain existing military functions, not a domain which was important in itself. There was no sense that space might become the 'high ground' of any future military confrontation and might therefore need to be controlled. And even if it was, this was something that could be left to the Americans. It is not surprising therefore that no significant attempts were made to establish and maintain a coherent British military space policy. Nor in the conventional wisdom was there any need for it. This was something that should be left to the two superpowers. MOD was not to be the champion of a British space policy, unlike its French equivalent.

Several other government departments and agencies have space responsibilities. The Department of Education and Sciences has a role in influencing research priorities and funding, including those of the Science and Engineering Research Council (SERC). SERC has long had a significant space science programme, costing £20 million in 1985/6, while other research councils have more limited, though important space concerns. The Meteorological Office, affiliated to the MOD and British signatory of Eumetsat, spends about £5 million a year on space services, now central to its main activities. As for the provision of communications services British Telecom International is the most important British agency and the designated signatory of and thus investor in Intelsat, Eutelsat and Inmarsat. Though its expenditure on space is not normally included in the totals for civilian expenditure on space, BTI has an investment of some £300 million in space services. Before privatization BTI was linked into the policy process through DTI and previously the Post Office. It has subsequently become a more independent actor and begun to acquire a more explicitly commercial philosophy. The Foreign and Commonwealth Office has a general role in advising on the international dimension, but no budgetary or programme responsibility.

But it was plain by the mid-eighties just how difficult it was to produce a coherent space policy with a secure funding base, when several departments were involved. This was to become even more of a problem as the development of space technologies began to produce services and applications relevant to yet other government departments, such as the Ministry of Agriculture, Fisheries and Food for crop forecasting or the Department of the Environment for monitoring environmental changes and so on. To stimulate user interest and also user investment proved quite a challenge within the established departmental structures. It was impossible for the Space

Branch of DTI to aggregate such diverse policy interests, especially when space technology was not even a top priority within DTI.

Science and technology policy

For over twenty years the British government has grappled with the problem of how best to formulate and implement policies with technological content. These are relevant to both domestic industry and international collaboration and raise issues about economic adjustment, international partnerships and competition and the political and security interests of the UK. Successive but not always successful experiments have been made with the mechanisms for policy management. None has yet produced a clear framework for either science or technology policies, or the connections between the two and industrial policy. The international complications have often proved daunting. The parameters of decision-making have also shifted, as government policy has altered on the respective roles of the private and public sectors. Space policy has been only one of many examples of drift and confusion in policy-making for science and technology, compounded by the sheer difficulty of comprehending what was at stake. As Richard Crossman noted sardonically in 1966 in his diary on the subject of the Black Arrow rocket launcher, 'How can Cabinet come to a sensible decision when none of us have the vaguest idea of what these things really are?' Ministers are generally ill-equipped to determine the guidelines of space policy. The systems used by Whitehall for garnering technical advice are imperfect and most officials have little grounding in the scientific and technical substance.

These inherent weaknesses in the policy process have long been the subject of criticism by the scientific establishment, commentators and parliament (especially the House of Lords and its Select Committee on Science and Technology). They have made for particular difficulties for the UK in negotiating with its international partners on many collaborative ventures. Three examples from recent events serve to illustrate the point. The debate over British participation in the European Airbus consortium has repeatedly involved tortuous deliberations within Whitehall and between Whitehall and industry. Proposals to extend the R&D programmes of the European Community have found Whitehall in several minds, a source of great irritation to Britain's European partners and the European Commission. Subscriptions to international scientific organizations, such as CERN, have repeatedly been victims or potential victims of financial squeezes and critical appraisal.

Irrespective of the space case, there has recently been a renewed effort by the government collectively to improve its grasp of decision making on R&D generally and issues of technology policy. One manifestation of this is the effort to strengthen the role and strategic functions of Cabinet procedures with a new Committee chaired by the Prime Minister and serviced by the secretariat in the Cabinet Office which deals with science and technology. Those involved have sought to extend this effort to cover more satisfactorily the international dimension. Other elements of the reforms include a commitment to improve the procedures for establishing a partnership with the scientific and industrial communities and to focus more coherently the priorities of the various research councils. The new Advisory Council on Science and Technology (ACOST), announced on 20 July 1987, is one indication of this. But to achieve greater effectiveness in this domain will require sustained determination and coherence far beyond what has been achieved hitherto.

Opaque decision-making
The British policy process is characteristically less transparent to outside scrutiny than those of most other Western democracies. This feature is all the more marked in areas with a high defence policy content. Policy and programmes are typically not widely discussed even in broad terms outside the executive and even within the executive the 'need to know principle' is vigorously pursued. Thus parliament, pressure groups, the media and public opinion are often ill-informed and poorly placed to offer constructive and focused criticism. Even basic facts may be hard to come by, such as the full range of government spending in space, military as well as civilian, since information is heavily classified. In the place of a broad public scrutiny there are, however, important and often informal networks of people who are drawn into a circle of consultation.

In the case of space policy there is an evident network of experts – scientists, technologists and industrialists – who regularly proffer advice on policy to government. But the network is closed and the policy community encapsulated. The advantage is that the network can operate swiftly and on a coordinated basis. The disadvantage is that it provides a further inhibition against wider debate, a special problem at a period when applications of space technology are beginning to open up on a much broader front. Though this weakness has been recognized by many of those involved, who well sense the need to build a broader basis of support and advice, the shift away from encapsulation is in practice hard to achieve.

The handicaps of incoherence

British space programmes had thus long been imprisoned in a culture and process which militated against the emergence of a strategic view. The fact that the programmes were so heavily international in orientation compounded rather than simplified the problems. British policy-makers had engaged in repeated international discussions and negotiations in the absence of a strategic national policy. So their effectiveness was severely impeded by the lack of clear policy guidelines.

This has produced a myriad of British weaknesses in the international arena. Within ESA the British government had got as far as recognizing the importance of its GNP-related share of the mandatory programmes and the subscription-related return from the applications programmes. But participation in the launcher programme was at best modest and by comparison with other major European countries feeble. But there was no policy base from which to derive a sharper focus. The industrial consequence was to lock British contractors into ESA's science programmes, many of which are long on innovation and short on commercial applications. Only in the field of communications satellites, happily very important in its own right, was there anything approaching a hard-nosed assertion of comparative advantage.

This did not, however, extend to a vigorous public promotion of British bids for the role of prime contractor in international tenders. The French, German and Italian governments have all had policies designed to foster for their preferred national contractors or consortia a serious stake in international contracts, and for that matter in contracts awarded nationally. British companies have been left much more to strive on the basis of their own efforts, which may have sharpened their commercial claws but has sometimes left them to bid on unequal terms in what are far from undistorted markets.

There was a marked antithesis between the heavily European orientation of Britain's civilian space programme and a reflexively

Atlanticist bent to the military space programme. There may be good and solid reasons of substance for this apparent dissonance, but questions as to the appropriateness of this bifurcated approach have not really surfaced. Hence the MOD has continued its policy of reliance on American collaboration, complemented by the national Skynet programme. Discussions with potential European partners, most plausibly the French, have been only tentative, and there has been no serious impetus to reexamine the merits of the case one way or another. This lacuna is all the more striking, given that within the British space industry there have emerged evident signs of dissatisfaction with some of the collaborative arrangements and terms of competition with US firms, along with anxiety about the future risks of dependence on US-set terms of access to technology and export controls.

Some of these difficulties reflect the absence of a strong foreign policy input into deliberations over British space programmes. It is not that the FCO has been anything less than supportive, but because space assets have not thus far been construed as vital attributes of Britain's international profile, the foreign policy dimension has been grafted on rather than helped set the parameters. Looked at in narrowly bureaucratic terms, it is also worthy of note that space issues are part of a disparate cluster of scientific and energy questions handled by one functional department within the FCO. The diplomats involved have been advisers on the modalities of international collaboration rather than the promoters of a considered view about preferred partners or the need for a particular international profile for Britain in space. Here again the British record diverges markedly from what can be observed in either analog European countries or in aspirant space powers elsewhere in the world. The creation of the BNSC has begun to change the picture a little, by giving the FCO an opportunity to voice a view on space policy as a whole as distinct from individual programmes or projects.

The quest for a new approach

It was precisely to cut through these imperfections of national policy-making and international engagement that the new BNSC was created in November 1985 as 'a focus for British space policy'. It was to 'improve the development of space technology' and achieve 'more effective policy coordination'. Its international orientation was secured by the appointment as first Director-General of Roy Gibson, former Director-General of ESA. He carried impeccable European credentials, as well as deep knowledge and experience of space programmes elsewhere.

BNSC became a semi-autonomous government agency, with an existence and profile to an extent independent of the rest of Whitehall. Its central staff (about 40 in number) were drawn substantially from the old Space Branch of the DTI but with an admixture of secondees from other departments, including the MOD and the FCO, and from industry. Its steering body and advisory boards included senior officials from across Whitehall as well as members of the industrial and scientific communities. Its responsibilities covered all the civilian space effort of DTI, the space activities of the research councils and some less classified defence work. The London headquarters of BNSC constitute the 'policy and programmes arm' charged with formulating policy and supervising programmes. Its 'technology arm' draws on some 240 staff in the Royal Aircraft Establishment at Farnborough (previously engaged on DTI funded research or MOD research of lower classification), and in the Rutherford-Appleton Laboratory at Chilton.

It is thus a bureaucratically complex animal, in that it has a separate persona but relies on collaborative arrangements with other research establishments of the government. It is charged with formulating strategy, but funding continues to be channelled through the pre-existing departmental budgets of DTI, and the Department of the Environment, along with SERC and the Meteorological Office. The funding for mainstream defence programmes in space remains firmly with MOD. As for ultimate political control, the route to the highest level of Cabinet decision-making was via a minister of state in DTI, who had parallel responsibilities in other areas of technology, but was not a full cabinet minister.

The first task of the top policy-makers in BNSC was to draft a strategic plan for the future of British space policy. This was achieved with creditable despatch by July 1986. The document, still not published, brought together the range of current and projected space programmes under both European and British umbrellas. It set them in the context of other international developments and the burgeoning of national space programmes of other countries. It drew attention to the rather modest level of British efforts to date and the limited returns that followed. It argued for a much more active national programme to develop and consolidate Britain's scientific and technological capabilites. It highlighted the important round of pending decisions in ESA and between ESA and Nasa, in which on past form British returns could only be limited. But, the document concluded, there was a real and perhaps fleeting opportunity for a quantum jump. With something like a two to threefold increase of investment (at the then prevailing estimated costs of new projects), the UK could expand its domestic programme and secure a very much more important stake in European space collaboration.

The document also vigorously deplored the historical biases of the British space programme. Because the level of the British effort had been relatively so modest, the only sensible option had been to channel the bulk of investment through ESA programmes. Without that basic effort in ESA, Britain would have had no serious impact or access to contracts, through which to develop space technologies. But the result was that the parallel national programme was tiny and very little margin was left for other international ventures. BNSC argued, using comparative examples, that there was a chicken and egg character to this. With a larger national programme Britain could also be a more effective European partner, have greater international impact and win a bigger return on investment for the British scientific and industrial communities. Furthermore Hotol, the design concept for a new launcher, might be a means of enlarging Britain's space capabilities in the launcher segment.

It was clear to those involved from the outset that these vigorously argued proposals covered only part of the subject. The BNSC plan ranged across civilian capabilities, but touched defence only indirectly. The hope was that a parallel review of Britain's military space effort would take place and then be dove-tailed with the civilian proposals. For many this was the crucial precondition of a fully coherent British space strategy in terms of R&D priorities, production capabilities, applications and international profile.

From proposals to decisions
So much for the carefully elaborated plan. BNSC's document, approved by Geoffrey Pattie, the minister responsible within DTI,

was ready for collective discussion by ministers. Of course some of the groundwork was already laid by consultations and deliberations between BNSC and various Whitehall departments, but a more formal and structured appraisal had to follow. And it was bound to be a difficult process for all of the reasons identified earlier in this chapter. Space policy was not going to be an easy subject for ministers to address. It would first have to be carefully explained that the BNSC was not advocating a quest for the moon and the stars, the realm of science fiction for most ministers, but a cool-headed nurturing of important technological and scientific assets. The financial costs were of course considerable and the Treasury had not been closely involved in the earlier discussions of substance. The military and civilian threads had to be properly drawn together. And the timing had to be right ... If this could be achieved the UK would have a well-honed new policy well ahead of the planned ESA ministerial meeting then scheduled for spring 1987.

In the event the timing went completely awry in both the UK and ESA, an interconnection which was initially merely an unhappy coincidence, though it came to imply linkages of substance. The normal British practice is for a specialized subject of this kind to go to Cabinet committee first and then to full Cabinet. It took many weeks for the BNSC plan to be judged 'ripe' for discussion by Cabinet committee. When it eventually rose up this ladder of decision-making, ministers were reluctant to reach a swift conclusion and the plan was referred back for an appraisal of its merits relative to those of similar technology subjects on which government decisions were pending and to other standing programmes of R&D investment. The defence elements took some months to emerge from lengthy deliberations within MOD.

The timetable for the key ESA ministerial slipped first from April to June and then to November 1987, thus removing what had been a powerful reason for speed. Moreover the delays in ESA resulted from several European governments having second and third thoughts about the commitments they had made in November 1985 to their joint long-term plan and from problems with some of the core components of the long-term plan. Negotiations between ESA and Nasa over the 'international space station' also dragged on. In the process the costings for the various collaborative projects were revised significantly upwards. The net result was to sow seeds of

51

greater doubt as to the reliability of any estimates for such complex projects. With closer study of the technical requirements for the international space station and the European ventures, notably Hermes and Ariane 5, it became evident that some redesign would be necessary and therefore that some of the proposals would not be fully achievable. Against the backcloth of an American space programme temporarily stalled by the Challenger disaster and problems with Ariane 3, the European launcher, it is easy to comprehend why those who were not space specialists had cause to question the logic of a major increase in British spending.

These delays stemmed from several independent sources, though of course they interacted with each other. But the net effect in the UK was to remove the momentum pressing for a decision. Instead there was no decision. BNSC was not asked to reformulate its strategic plan, though its initial estimates were already overtaken by a further year's events, a development clearly identified by BNSC to ministers. Although ministers did not collectively decide to endorse the plan, they did not reject it either. In the absence of a clear policy steer the Prime Minister simply announced in July 1987 that policy would stay for the time being as before and funding would remain constant. It was only after the implications became evident both from internal discussions within government and in response to the rather remarkable public outcry articulated through the press (during the summer parliamentary recess) that the DTI announced that a modest extra sum (about £4 million) would after all be available. This would keep British options open as regards the forward plans of ESA, and leave some scope for reappraisal as the international negotiations proceeded in ESA and with Nasa. British Aerospace and Rolls-Royce also reaffirmed their commitment to provide interim funding for Radarsat and the Hotol study, even though they could not be sure of longer-term funding. In the process the British government had begun to be blamed, at least in the public commentary, as a critical source of the emerging problems within ESA. The truth of the matter was different in some crucial respects. ESA's difficulties were partly a result of genuine technological and design constraints with the new projects and their cost effects and thereby the consequential heart-searching in many other European capitals. But the risks were clear: either Britain could become the easy scapegoat for any subsequent reneging by ESA as a whole; or other

ESA members, led by France and Germany, would forge ahead, leaving the UK on the starting blocks.

The roots of indecision

The new BNSC plan had become trapped in circumstances and pressures all too familiar from the history of Britain's previous involvement in international space collaboration. Need it have been so? The answer lies with two different factors. First, with hindsight (always easier than foresight) it is possible to identify ways in which the process of decision-making could have been more skilfully managed. But second, the whole story illustrates continuing structural flaws in the way in which the British government deals with the interfaces between domestic and international policies.

BNSC was set up as a semi-autonomous agency with only partial responsibility for space policy and no firm power base. Many such British agencies have found themselves floundering in the past when faced with established departmental baronies and fierce financial scrutiny from the Treasury. The Director-General had no hot-line to the Cabinet and the indirect route through a minister of state is not an easy one, factors which have more to do with the culture of Whitehall than with the personalities and talents of the office holders. Decisions on new policy strategies need powerful and determined advocates inside the main Cabinet room. During the period of non-decision there were no such advocates. The DTI went through a prolonged period of changes in Secretaries of State, each of whom was simultaneously burdened by many other tricky policy issues. The MOD had plenty of other issues on which to do battle in Cabinet and for understandable reasons of its own was not likely to provide the determined advocacy required. Perhaps a different minister might have treated the subject differently. But of those recently in office Michael Heseltine was perhaps the only one who had developed a strong personal interest in space, a legacy of the period in which ESA itself was created and Britain, after some hesitation, became a founding member. And however important the international dimension, vigorous support from the FCO could not be a sufficient catalyst for a costly strategy with far-ranging industrial and security facets.

The initial attribution of responsibilities to BNSC to some extent determined the effectiveness of its remit. It was a major step to aggregate the responsibilities for civilian space policy and to link them firmly to operational programmes and research facilities. Already that constituted a qualitative improvement on the previously dispersed character of policy formulation and management. But this did not lead directly to the full alignment of the civilian and military dimensions for which the critics of the *status quo ante* had hoped. BNSC has been able to make considerable headway in the exchange of information and assessment of the two dimensions and this represents a significant improvement. But in the less than two years since its creation BNSC has not been able to take the subsequent steps necessary for policy integration in terms of political direction, conceptual focus or a single source of funding. Again in retrospect this is not surprising. Experience from many other areas of British government illustrates the inhibitions on making such a shift, especially when they involve the acquisition of substantive responsibilities from within so central an area of policy as is commanded by MOD and one which deals with such sensitive issues. It may be small comfort to the BNSC, but this difficulty is also shared by their counterparts elsewhere. In the USA Nasa and the DoD have lived with an uneasy demarcation of responsibilities. Even the powerful and long-established CNES in France has not entirely resolved the question of how to handle the civilian-military boundaries.

Similar problems arise over budgetary responsibilities. The holder of a budget is always more strongly placed than the claimant on someone else's budget. BNSC acquired policy responsibilities but not full budgetary control of civilian space expenditure, which has remained divided amongst existing departmental budgets. For a government committed to reducing, not expanding, public expenditure overall and to keeping the R&D budget constant, larger civilian expenditure in space has to be found from compensating savings elsewhere. This means that those departments which are the relevant budget holders have to be prepared to forgo some of their other commitments. In particular for space this would have required the DTI to accept that space merited more and some of its other technology programmes less, just as an increase in expenditure on military space would require the MOD to forgo something else.

To establish the hierarchy of priorities in practice requires great adroitness in negotiations within Whitehall and vis-à-vis the Treasury. A task-oriented agency such as the BNSC has the strength of being able to focus on its allocated domain, in a way which is very hard to achieve as only one division within a large department. It can try to enunciate the merits of its case with clarity and precision, as BNSC sought to do in its strategic plan. But such an agency has few bargaining counters to use in inter-departmental negotiation. And it is rare in negotiations in any context for the merits of the case to suffice, unless they are firmly attached to an overriding national goal and specific national interests, as they have been in French space policy.

Hence BNSC was always bound to be vulnerable to Treasury questioning. To achieve 'success' vis-à-vis the Treasury is peculiarly difficult in the British system, for reasons adduced earlier in this chapter. In the space case the difficulties were compounded by the continuing debate within government about the relative roles of public and private investors in technology. BNSC was caught in an intractable dilemma. If it argued that space technologies offered really good and profitable returns on investment, then surely this must be obvious to private investors too, in which case *why* not shift some of the investment burden out of the public sector? If, on the other hand, the space industry was not likely in the short term to be viable from its own and private investors' resources, did it really merit scarce government expenditure?

BNSC quite reasonably opted to put a mixed and balanced assessment, arguing that public investment now could be followed after a period by willing private investment. To this the industry added that it was not seeking full government subsidy, since the companies involved were already dipping quite deeply into their own pockets. But the case is not an easy one to express convincingly. It happens also to be the case that the BNSC was not able to draw on well-developed economic analyses to support its arguments on this front. Again the problem is not peculiar to the British, but well known to counterparts in most other European countries. It would be asking the impossible to expect any economist to produce a cast-iron evaluation of the profitability and returns of investment in space over the medium term.

BNSC's reappraisal of space strategy was in the event peculiarly unlucky in its timing. The plan reached ministers just as several apparently similar proposals demanded a decision from government. The Alvey programme, Britain's major initiative in information technology, was reaching the review stage. The next round of funding for the European Airbus had to be agreed, involving British Aerospace as a major player. The European Community had on its negotiating table a series of proposals for a new framework programme for R&D across a range of technology sectors. Participating countries were also being asked to make their pledges. A long-simmering debate about military R&D was reaching boiling point. The advocates of continued and substantial British involvement in each of these areas were making their cases, inevitably to an extent in competition with each other. But there were no agreed yardsticks for ranking their relative merits.

The international ramifications of all these were considerable, even of Alvey, the only specifically domestic programme. Each of the others was handled by a different international agency or consortium, sometimes several in the case of military R&D, with collaborative elements. So the international dimension had no unifying role, in contrast, for example, to the way in which disparate policy areas affected by the EC are pulled forcefully together by the British government operating collectively. On the contrary each of the European cases – Airbus (A330 and A340), the EC's framework programme and the ESA elements of British space policy – pulled in a different direction, with diverse collateral complications. But it is also relevant that of these various European frameworks ESA was by far the least well known inside and outside government. It is not only that space policy as such had not a broadly based constituency, but ESA's track record was barely acknowledged by the 'Europeanists' within the UK.

To this catalogue of obstacles should be added a more general impediment. Sophisticated though the British policy process may be, it has been peculiarly deficient in identifying strategies in many policy areas, domestic and external. The British inherited strength lies in edging towards adjustments in policy and in a sense of rationalizing the inevitable. A central plank in the governing style of Mrs Thatcher has been to reform precisely this feature of British policy-making, hence the deliberate 'radicalism' of much of what she has sought to achieve. But this reformist spirit has not yet penetrated the whole of British government. The initiative to create BNSC was itself a step towards reaching space policy, but the follow-through has not yet emerged. Amongst the free marketeers only the Adam Smith Institute was advocating increased public spending on space.

Several other countries have taken a more strategic view of space policy. Within Europe the best-known case is France, not always a congenial comparator. But the British have something to learn from other European partners. The German government has been groping towards a more activist national space policy and a role and influence in European space policy which would secure a larger industrial return, a foothold in collective security capabilities and a more visible presence in the international arena. The Italians have steadily expanded their public investment in space and overtaken the British, because they believe that a modern technological nation with aspirations to international influence cannot forgo the acquisition of substantial space assets. The Swedes have shrewdly developed impressive national capabilities which complement their ESA contribution and serve defined national policy goals.

It follows that to achieve the strategic view sought by BNSC and the British space policy community requires either a wider revolution in the British policy process or so powerful a jolt that space issues acquire a compelling political salience. As this paper went to press the future of Britain's space policy awaited a final decision as part of the current review of all publicly funded R&D. This was being carried out by the new Advisory Council on Science and Technology, established in August 1987, and the revised and strengthened procedures within the Cabinet system – both aimed at achieving more strategic policy. The hope was that a decision would emerge in time for the meeting of ESA ministers scheduled for November 1987.

5

THE POLICY ISSUES

Four scenarios can be envisaged for Britain's future in space. The first is the *significant expansion* advocated by BNSC in its strategy document and endorsed throughout the space policy community in the UK. This would yield a larger national programme, a more proactive international role and bring Britain into line with the other major European countries. A second scenario is to be *serious but selective*, that is to increase investment and target it at chosen priority areas, which could include a mix of national and collaborative activities. A third possibility is the *status quo*, predicated on the retention of the current level and pattern of expenditure, but almost certain in practice to mean a decline in real terms. It could well lead to a fourth scenario in which Britain became a *user not producer* of space technologies, relying on sources of supply and innovation from outside the UK.

Reaching a critical threshold
Experience suggests that a critical threshold separates the user from the effective producer. The latter to be credible needs not only appropriate human skills and production capabilities of high quality, but also a public policy commitment and a willingness to dedicate resources on a sustained basis. Beneath that threshold the options likely to be available for both R&D and production will be narrow. They would probably justify a small public budget concentrated on the support of a few areas of niche production and the stimulus of specialized user demand. Above the critical threshold a

far wider range of options is available from the selective to the more comprehensive. Selection has to depend on choices about the relative balance of national and collaborative activities, with reference to several policy arenas beyond the space sector. The experiences of other countries and the advice of space specialists in the UK broadly combine to suggest that the critical threshold in the future will lie above the level of British commitments to space in recent years. The *status quo* is in other words less than the phrase suggests. The British space community has achieved as much as it has because of a mixture of factors: inherited scientific and technological ability; flair and determination in parts of the industry; the legacy of the ESA package deal of the mid-seventies; and a privileged transatlantic connection. But it will be difficult to sustain these favourable conditions in the next decade and beyond without a further injection of effort and investment.

Thus the choice of policy requires a sharp appraisal of where British interests lie. It is the contention of this paper that these are not simply questions about R&D policy. British interests in space should be assessed in terms of the relevance of:

– a capacity for innovation and application in an area of technology and science with wide-ranging impacts;
– the resilience and competitiveness of the British space industry;
– access to influence on discussions of the international space regime of the future;
– international partnerships in Europe and with the USA;
– linkages with other arenas of European and transatlantic collaboration; and
– aspirations to global political influence.

The price of dependence
Judgments about the relative weight of these interests have to recognize that there is no option of independence in any of the imaginable scenarios for British space policy. The *user not producer* scenario implies heavy dependence on the rest of the world, with the parameters and substance determined elsewhere. Service-providers could survive with a good chance of being competitive but with imported technology.

Both *status quo* and *serious but selective* scenarios would be built on a degree of dependence shading into interdependence. The *significant expansion* scenario is the only one which would give either the British government or the British industry the opportunity really to define some of the terms of international collaboration.

The prerequisites of partnership

The extent to which collaboration is a crucial component of any space policy makes it especially important to take account of the prerequisites of partnership. What Britain gets out of collaboration in space will be determined in large measure by what Britain is prepared to put into collaboration in terms of expertise, markets and commitment as well as resources. The British record is in this respect not entirely favourable. A cool-headed assessment has to recognize that in some fields – scientific advance, telecommunications and some specialized niches – Britain has contributed substantially to and gained from international collaboration and the development of Europe's collective capabilities. But against that has to be set a perception elsewhere in Europe that Britain has had an ambivalent presence in space, a perception that is based on some solid evidence.

But collaboration is not the whole story of international space relations. It is also about access to assets and competition for position. Space activities (for both producers and users) depend on access to assets held elsewhere: launch facilities, key technologies or know-how, contracts and markets. Any British government which wants some national security capability in space has to recognize this, and so do British producers and users of space technology. A robust space policy must have as an objective the pursuit of an effective scientific, technological and industrial base, which necessarily entails a competitive toughness. International relations in space, if they are to serve British interests, have thus to yield a well-judged balance of collaboration and competition.

Policy has to recognize too the tensions between nationalism and internationalism. ESA has many strengths but it also reveals the competing national preferences of its members. There is no European security policy in space not least because different national philosophies and assessments of military need persist. The United States has been a valuable partner of the UK, but it has many different and perhaps diverging interests in the security field and commercial domain. Thus far British space policy has lacked the sharp definition of national interests which has characterized the approach of Britain's main partners and competitors.

The risks

Space science and technology are still immature. Only in the communications sector are there the characteristics of a relatively mature industry with established customers. Only in the provision of the ground infrastructure is there anything like a 'normal' market in operation, already heavily penetrated by Japanese exports. The remaining range of space activities depends on an assertion of belief that maturity will follow and in its train economic, social and political benefits. These arguments may well be correct but they cannot be proven. Policy-makers thus have to reach their conclusions through an assessment of risk. In the British context this ties a huge millstone around the neck of the advocates. Space projects are necessarily expensive and usually technologically speculative, a perfect recipe for scepticism as to their value in the British policy culture.

But this is not the only risk. It may well be that space will become much more important not just in terms of technology and the practical applications, but as a vehicle of political power. The international system is not static. Prudent insurance provision in the fields of foreign and security policies may be desirable and suggest that Britain cannot afford to forgo the opportunity to maintain a serious level of space capability, but the premium is also expensive. What is evident is that the actuarial evaluation can be made only by calculating both military and civilian costs and benefits. With this in view the defence budget announced by the French government for 1988 significantly identifies the space sector (alongside nuclear and conventional) as a necessary area of expansion for which an 80 per cent increase of budget is planned.

Who then should bear the risks? The public purse or private capital? Or both? And on what basis? Since at the end of the day the level of British commitment to space has to be reflected in resources allocated on a long-term basis, the question of money cannot be avoided. This is in no sense to reduce the arguments to narrow accounting criteria. In no country have investments in space been able to flow from private capital until the stage at which particular customers can be identified and captured, though of course the industry already draws on some private investors and company assets. It makes perfectly good economic sense to press in the direction of larger private funding. But in the interim governments, including the British, cannot avoid making some public investment too.

Accurate figures are hard to come by, but it is probably the case at the moment that in the civilian space field in the UK there is approximate parity of investment by the public and private sectors across the space and ground segments. This profile of investment is a good starting point and compares well with other countries. Future policy (at whatever level) would need to rest on a continued partnership of public and private investment. But it would be an illusion to expect the balance between the two to shift dramatically towards the private sector until the degree of risk is diminished. One further complication is that the opportunity costs of opting in or out of space activities cannot be quantified. The arguments have to stand or fall on delicate qualitative evaluation.

National, European and transatlantic dimensions

British space activities have been and are likely to remain three-legged, based on national, European and American elements. For other ESA members the transatlantic dimension has become rather more of a stimulus to emulation. Britain has a small national programme in the civilian and military fields, a useful civilian involvement in ESA and a substantial military reliance on US sources in lieu of direct British involvement to support a global foreign policy and nuclear capabilities. So far the three legs have been able to support a reasonably balanced programme, but their continued solidity cannot be taken for granted. Moreover BNSC has argued, with some support from elsewhere, that Britain has suffered from the small scale of the national programme. It has not produced the range and depth of activities which would be necessary to ensure future access to innovation and effective application of space technologies. Thus a cornerstone of the BNSC proposal for a *significant expansion* was an expanded national programme to serve

British economic, technological and scientific interests. It would also enable Britain to become a more effective member of ESA and derive more in the future from the envisaged expansion of European programmes. Enhanced capabilities could subsequently be harnessed for security purposes as well. Of course there is a problem about the costs of a larger European effort. ESA's long-term programme is very ambitious and will be expensive, probably above the current forecasts. European governments have taken a view that they cannot afford to stand still and that by identifying collaboration they can share both the risks and the benefits of expansion.

The *status quo* scenario would be likely to produce a still greater share of the British civilian effort being consumed by ESA and even then concentrated in only some ESA programmes. Current levels of expenditure would not enable the UK to participate seriously in all of the new optional programmes. Nor would the status quo easily permit the retention of the national capabilities which would be needed should security interests and technological developments begin to weigh the arguments in favour of a larger military space programme, either nationally or in a European context. The *serious but selective* scenario would leave some of these options open. With some increase in resources Britain could both extend the national civilian programme in target areas and be actively engaged in several ESA programmes. Sufficient strength might well be acquired to facilitate robustness in parts of space industry, some of which could be mobilized, if necessary, for an expansion of security programmes.

But these questions of national versus European balance cannot be assessed in isolation. The US is likely to remain the dominant space power in the West. But British and American interests may not always coincide as closely as in the past. It is already clear that American industrial and commercial policy is assertive. American warnings on strategic export controls have so far prevented European payloads from being launched on Soviet rockets. The Americans have not been easy negotiating partners in the discussion of the international space station. A more active ESA might well find itself more assertive vis-à-vis the USA. Moreover changes in the context of European security are already provoking much more vigorous discussion of ways to develop a collective European capability. The consequential pressures on Britain are likely to be considerable. Over the medium term it will be increasingly difficult to avoid making a choice between the current mix of European and transatlantic connections and a more European orientation.

A window of opportunity

British space policy has reached a crucial moment. Decisions currently being prepared in London, within ESA and between the USA and ESA will determine whether or not Britain emerges as a weighty space power and how much headroom there is for further exploitation of space technologies for both civilian and security purposes. To be credible with a depth of expertise, a sound industrial base and the ability to deploy effective international influence requires investment well beyond current levels. The critical threshold is the *serious but selective* scenario. Judgments as to whether to go beyond in the direction proposed by BNSC would be easier to reach if the defence-related side of the coin had been a more visible component of the debate. For this reason it would be an advantage if the defence and civilian sides moved more closely together within the policy process in Whitehall.

Nor will the window of opportunity be open for long if ESA succeeds in turning its framework plan into a substantive programme up to the year 2000. Once the new ESA package deal is agreed it will set for many years the terms of European civilian collaboration and the distribution of industrial work shares and benefits.

Though much of the work of the space industry is conducted outside ESA, it has so far relied heavily on experience gained in ESA programmes. Britain cannot expect to retain an effective capability in space at the current level of engagement. It is of course possible to opt out and to rely on developed technology from elsewhere. But it must be recognized that this is not simply a choice about just another area of R&D. Space has far-reaching implications for British economic modernization as well as for Britain's foreign and security policies.

STATISTICAL APPENDIX
TO CHAPTER 2

Table 1   British civilian expenditure on space (in £m)

Year	ESA	National	Total
1972/3	5.4	12.8	18.2
1973/4	11.1	11.4	22.5
1974/5	19.6	11.5	31.1
1975/6	29.1	16.1	45.2
1976/7	38.3	16.3	54.6
1977/8	39.6	14.9	54.5
1978/9	39.8	13.1	52.9
1979/80	42.4	13.9	56.3
1980/1	49.3	13.9	63.2
1981/2	62.3	15.9	78.2
1982/3	64.3	17.3	81.6
1983/4	65.1	20.6	85.7
1984/5	73.1	20.7	93.8
1985/6	83.2	23.0	106.2
1986/7	78.9	37.1	116.0

Source: BNSC.

Table 2   British expenditure in 1986/7 by programme area (in £m)

	ESA	National	Total	Source
Civilian				
Columbus	4.4	0.6	5.0	DTI
Communications	30.0[a]	1.6	31.6	DTI
Earth observation	15.4[b]	21.0	36.4	DTI, SERC, Met O, NERC
General budget	5.4	–	5.4	DTI, SERC, MOD, OGDs[c]
Ground facilities	–	0.3	0.3	DTI
Microgravity	0.3	–	0.3	DTI, SERC
Launchers	8.7	0.7	9.4	DTI
Science	14.7	6.2	20.9	SERC, DTI, MOD, OGDs
Technology	–	6.7	6.7	DTI, MOD
Total	78.9	37.1	116.0	
Military	–	c.100.0	c.100.0	MOD
Total civilian and military			c.216.0	

[a] Of which £19m on Olympus.
[b] Of which £11m on ERS-1.
[c] Other government departments.

Table 3 International comparisons of expenditure in 1985

Country	European accounting units (million)
USSR	27,288.5
USA	19,927.4
China (est.)	3,000.0
Europe (ESA + national)	1,778.9
France	692.7
Japan	635.0
Germany	361.3
Italy	186.7
UK	165.3
India	156.9
Canada	156.6

Note: US, Soviet and Chinese figures include high military spending. European figures cover only civilian public expenditure.

Table 4 British national satellites and vehicles

Ariel 1	1962	Scientific
Ariel 2	1964	Scientific
Ariel 3	1967	Scientific (first wholly British satellite)
Ariel 4	1971	Scientific
Ariel 5	1974	Scientific
Ariel 6	1979	Scientific
X-4 (Miranda)	1974	Experimental
UoSat 1	1981	Experimental—Ham radio
UoSat 2	1984	Experimental—Ham radio
UKS	1984	Scientific
Skynet 1	1969	Military Comsat
Skynet 1B	1970	Military Comsat/failed in orbit
Skynet 2A	1974	Military Comsat/launch failure
Skynet 2B	1974	Military Comsat
Skynet 4	1987	Military Comsat/launch pending
Black Arrow	1969–71	Launcher

Statistical appendix to Chapter 2

Table 5   British involvement in European programmes

Country	% contribution to ESA – 1986	% workshare in Ariane 4
France	27.2	57.0
Germany	24.4	18.2
Italy	15.0	6.9
UK	13.1	3.7
Belgium	3.9	4.6
Other ESA	15.9	9.6

Table 6   The British primary space industry: a profile

British Aerospace	Space systems, sub-systems, satellites, launcher design
Ferranti	Inertial systems for rockets and satellites, ground stations
Logica	Software engineering, image processing, data communications
Marconi Communications Systems	Ground stations, terminals, associated systems
Marconi Space Systems	Space systems, satellites, ground stations
Plessey	Ground stations for telecommunications
Racal Decca	Navigation systems, ground terminals
Software Sciences	Software
Standard Telephones and Cables	Marine communications and studies
Thorn-EMI	Components for space and ground segments

Note: About 100 companies in all are involved in the design and manufacture of space systems and ground infrastructure.

Table 7 Satellites with British prime contractors (since 1971)

Satellite	Launch date	Customer	Prime contractor	Description
Nato 4	(1990, first of 2)	Nato	BAe/MSS	Military communications
Inmarsat 2	(1988, first of 3)	INMARSAT	BAe	Second generation maritime communications
Olympus	(1987)	ESA	BAe	Second generation communications technology-proving
Skynet 4	(1988, first of 3)	UK/MOD	BAe	UK military communications
Giotto	1985	ESA	BAe	Halley's Comet interception
ECS-1,2,4,5	1983 1984 1987	ESA	BAe	European communications
Marecs A,B2	1981 1984	ESA	BAe	Maritime communications
Ariel 6	1979	UK/SERC	MSS	Heavy elements in cosmic radiation: X-ray astronomy
OTS-2	1978	ESA	BAe	European communications technology-proving
GEOS 1,2	1977 1978	ESA	BAe	Particles and fields in magnetosphere
Skynet 2B	1974	UK/MOD	MSS	UK military communications
Ariel 5	1974	UK/SRC	MSS	X-ray astronomy
X4 (Miranda)	1974	UK/DTI	BAe	Technology-proving (3-axis stabilization)
ESRO 4	1972	ESRO	BAe	Ionospheric solar particles and lower magnetosphere
Ariel 4	1971	UK/SRC	BAe	Ionospheric measurements and particle experiment
X3 (Prospero)	1971	UK/DTI	RAE	Technology-proving

Source: United Kingdom Industrial Space Committee.

Table 8   Industrial partnerships in Europe

Country	Consortia		
	Cosmos	Mesh	Star
Belgium	ETCA		
France	Aerospatiale SAT	Matra	Thomson
Germany	MBB-Erno	MBB-Erno	Dornier
Italy	Selenia-Spazio	Aeritalia	Fiat
Netherlands		Fokker	
Spain	Casa	Inter	Sener
Sweden		Saab	Ericsson
Switzerland			Contraves
UK	MSS	BAe	BAe

Table 9   International contracts: Inmarsat 2, approximate industrial participation

Country	Contractor	% participation	% contribution
UK	BAe	34	14.5
USA	Hughes	46	30.7
France	Matra	12	1.7
Netherlands		3	2.3
Japan		2	7.0
Germany		1	1.7
Italy		1	1.9
Spain		1	1.2
Other members		0	39.0

Table 10   International contracts: Intelsat 6, actual participation
for first five spacecraft

Company	Participation	$m	% work	% contribution
Hughes and other USA	Prime contractor	384.0	72.8	24.1
British Aerospace (UK)	Cradle/carrier—separation clamps, C & K band reflectors, C band horns, Spacecraft structure and harness	32.8	6.2	13.2
Thomson CSF (France)	K band TWTs and receivers, C band receivers and multiplexers	24.8	4.7	5.9
Selenia (Italy)	Digital telemetry, TT & C transponder, C & K band global antennas, bicone antenna, K band spot beam antennas, telemetry global horn	24.4	4.6	5.9
NEC (Japan)	K band receivers, master oscillators, up converters, solid state power amplifiers	22.5	4.3	3.1
Spar (Canada)	C band receivers, driver amplifiers, EPCs TWTAs integration	18.1	3.4	2.5
MBB (Germany)	Solar arrays, substrates, complete solar panels 16.2	} 20.6	3.9	3.6
Telefunken (Germany)	Solar cell CICs 4.4			

Total 527.2

Table 11   Launch vehicles and British contractors

Project	Customer	Prime contractor	Sub-systems	Description
Europa (1st stage)	ELDO	BAe	Marconi Ferranti	Guidance computer Gyroscopes. Inertial guidance.
Black Arrow	UK/DTI	BHC	Royal Ordnance Ferranti	3rd stage fuel motor. Gyroscopes
Ariane	ESA/ Arianespace	CNES (France)	Ferranti Marconi BAe	Inertial sensing system. On-board software. Flight control unit. Release gear and structures. Spelda double launch system.
Delta/Titan/ Saturn/Thor	Nasa		TEE	Inertial guidance packages.
Space Shuttle	Nasa		TEE	High reliability inertial systems; cabin pressure monitoring; hydraulic degassers and fluid purifiers; hybrid element potentiometers in flight indicators.

Source: United Kingdom Industrial Space Committee.